To Brooke —
with much affection +
admiration for a fellow author!
Much love, Jen
xo

Overdue
Assignment

Taking Responsibility
for Canada's Schools

Jennifer Lewington
Graham Orpwood

John Wiley & Sons

Toronto • New York • Chichester • Brisbane • Singapore

John Wiley & Sons Canada Limited
22 Worcester Road
Rexdale, Ontario
M9W 1L1

Canadian Cataloguing in Publication Data

Lewington, Jennifer, 1949–
    Overdue assignment : taking responsibility for
Canada's schools

1. Education – Canada.   2. Educational change –
Canada.   I. Orpwood, Graham W. F., 1942–   .
II. Title.

LA412.L49   1993   370'.971   C93-093930-1

Production Credits
Jacket design: Michael Gray/First Image
Jacket photo: Gabe Palmer/Masterfile
Text design: JAQ
Printer: John Deyell Company

Printed and bound in Canada
10 9 8 7 6 5 4 3 2 1

To my parents,
Jean and the late Peter Lewington,
who taught me the most important lessons of life.

— Jennifer Lewington

Contents

Preface

S*chool reform is* on everyone's lips, but the issues and implications deserve careful thought that leads to considered action. To date, however, Canadians have watched as the education community and its critics talk past one another from their fixed positions. Canadians deserve better.

Our motivation in writing *Overdue Assignment* is very simple: to promote a more fruitful public discussion about school reform in Canada. While there is much that is good about Canada's elementary and secondary schools, there is also much that could be better. Our aim is to spur, prod and provoke Canadians to think in new ways about their schools. In the process, we hope the public and the education community itself can learn to speak a common language about their expectations — and how these can best be fulfilled in the interest of all students. The search for that common language is elusive: schools are separated from their communities by the professional jargon of education and other unnecessary barriers to effective communication between parents, students and teachers. Decoding the language is one of the essential steps towards a healthier debate. Only when the terms of discussion are clearer will schools and their communities be able to meet on common ground.

In times of uncertainty, the temptation is to reach for simple answers to complex questions. In education, the risk is even greater because the stakes are so high — our children's future. There is no simple answer for what is wrong with our schools, but the solutions are not beyond the reach of Canadians. We have tried to create a frame of reference within which to examine the strengths and weaknesses of the current education system and to explore the potential for improvements. Demystifying the politics of education is another necessary step towards a healthy debate; with that comes a willingness to sort out fact from fiction. Only when there is a greater understanding of the issues involved will schools and their communities be able to co-operate in a genuine partnership.

Canadians have good reason to expect a lot of their schools. By almost any yardstick, Canada has the people and the resources to deliver an education system second to none. Yet many Canadians are losing faith in the ability of their schools to provide the necessary survival tools for the next generation. If Canadians are to renew their faith in public education, and that is essential, they will have to ask more of their schools — and themselves.

It is too easy just to criticize the performance of schools today. The more challenging, and ultimately rewarding, job is to get involved in solutions that will help all students and schools do better. Every Canadian has a role to play, whether as a voter, or a volunteer. In so doing, everyone must demonstrate a willingness to understand the issues and get involved in the solutions. Taking responsibility for Canada's schools begins at home — but extends to all members of the community. It is an overdue assignment, but one worth the effort.

While there is certainly cause for concern, there are also grounds for optimism. Across Canada, there are schools already engaged in the kind of listening, adapting and experimenting that we urge in this book. Unfortunately, these examples are few and far between, and deserve much wider exposure. Our hats are off to all those parents, teachers and schools who have embarked on innovative projects to meet the diverse needs of students. To those who have their success stories, we would like to hear from you about what works — and why. Please write to us: c/o Professional, Reference and Trade Division, John Wiley and Sons Canada Limited, 22 Worcester Road, Rexdale, Ontario, M9W 1L1.

Acknowledgements

*A*s authors, we approached the challenge of writing this book with some trepidation because of our different backgrounds and skills. One of us has spent his professional career in education. The other has spent her professional life in journalism, with a long-time involvement in education. Nevertheless, it proved to be a very rewarding relationship. We worked well as a team, bringing different perspectives to bear on the difficult issues. Like all Canadians who care about improving the education system, we have had to confront our own biases, to understand those of the other and to have honest disagreements — all with a view to finding new resolutions to old conflicts. Though our names appear in alphabetical order, ours is a joint project in every sense of the word.

We have been the fortunate recipients of help and advice from numerous sources, without whom our project could not have been completed. Graham Orpwood appreciates the contributions of:

associates at The Impact Group, especially Ron Freedman, Jeffrey Crelinsten, Robert Fripp and John de la Mothe; colleagues at York University Faculty of Education; and long-time friend and mentor Douglas Roberts. Jennifer Lewington is most grateful to *The Globe and Mail* for a leave of absence to complete the book. As well, a large debt of thanks goes to family and friends who graciously agreed to read the manuscript and offered helpful comments. In addition, our work has benefited from the active interest and support of many parents, teachers, ministry officials and university faculty who took part in interviews.

From the beginning, the enthusiastic interest and support of John Wiley and Sons Canada has stimulated and encouraged us. In particular, we wish to thank Julia Woods and Karen Milner for their commitment, patience and good humour. In the editing stage, we have benefited enormously from the thoughtful comments and suggestions of Jennifer Glossop and Wendy Thomas. As the manuscript took shape, Mary Lynn Smith and Barbara Kilbourn assisted with research, fact-checking and illustrations.

Last, but not least, we could not have carried on the project without the love and support of our respective spouses, George Pearson and Sylvia Orpwood. They have read manuscripts, offered critical commentary, prepared marvellous dinners and, in more ways that can ever be enumerated, been full and active partners in the enterprise. However, errors of omission and commission remain those of the authors.

Chapter 1

Voices in Conflict

*P*ublic education faces a crisis of confidence in the 1990s. The unease, doubt and even anger over the state of schools today reflect a general loss of faith in public institutions and officials in Canada. Like the divisive battle over free trade in the late 1980s and the exhausting, inconclusive wrangles over the Constitution in the early 1990s, the fight over education is emotionally charged, polarized and deeply personal. And no wonder, because the stakes are so high. When schools fall short, the country pays the cost in human terms: squandered opportunities for young people to reach for the best in themselves and thereby contribute fully to Canadian society.

The dissonant voices in education — some raising the alarm, others growing cynical — signal an erosion of public trust and respect for those traditionally responsible for the schools: the politicians, the policy makers and the teachers. Complaints about the cost of education, the number of school drop-outs, inequities faced by linguistic and racial minorities, teaching philosophy and practice, mediocre student performance on international tests and graduates ill-equipped for an increasingly complex world of work are the cracks in a system under stress. In the 1990s, Canadians are worried about losing out competitively in a world beyond their control. As the country moves from a bruising recession into a jobless recovery, the public looks to education as the currency of economic security. In their fear of losing ground to others, parents expect elementary and secondary schools to provide the knowledge and skills that will give their children an edge in tackling the uncertainties ahead. Increasingly, though, Canadians ask if schools are delivering the goods, either now or for the future. The public system as we have known it is being called to account.

But on whose terms? The battlefield of education has armies of interest groups. Politicians, bureaucrats, school board trustees, school administrators, teachers, parents, students, workers and employers, each group with its own agenda, are determined to wage the campaign on their terms. However, no single interest can claim a full view of the field nor speak with one voice for all its perceived constituents. As a group, parents are no more homogeneous than teachers or employers. Moreover, the tension over whose voice should be heard is exacerbated by differences between older Canadians and those who still have children in school. The dawning reality of chronic government deficits is that education must fight for scarce resources in a political environment where the aging baby-boom generation increasingly will demand a shift in services from schools to health care and related programs for the elderly. As a result, schools will be under intense pressure to demonstrate their effectiveness in delivering quality results for students and the system as a whole.

In the cacophony of complaints, allegations and counter-charges, the public is understandably confused about what is really wrong with education and what remedies should be administered. In the 1990s, the uncertainty is heightened by a clash of ideologies, values and expectations about schools; for example, is education primarily a tool of economic renewal, a force for social justice or an exercise in character building? The answer varies according to the interest group. Moreover, all the disagreements carry a political subtext. For instance, the discord over what to teach students and how to teach them is nominally an issue of pedagogy. In reality, it is a power struggle over who controls the classroom. Similarly, friction over testing and evaluation has its roots in public pressure for accountability — for schools to show what they do and how well they do it. The political sub-theme is whose voice counts most in setting the agenda for education.

The conflicts in education have shaken the confidence of Canadians in their schools. In early 1993, in a survey of 1,507 Canadians, Angus Reid/Southam News found that nearly one-half (46 per cent) of those polled believed that the quality of education is worse today than twenty-five years ago.[1] The impression left by this and other public opinion surveys on education is that Canadian schools are in free-fall descent, doing little or nothing to improve quality. Paradoxically, schools are in a state of turmoil and change even as they seek to address contradictory expectations and demands from all the interest groups in education. In spite of honest efforts by many of the traditional players — the teachers, school administrators and policy makers — the conflict in education is, if anything, marked by growing public cynicism. For all the sound, motion and activity of reform, there is little satisfaction in the process nor much evidence that the core conflicts that bedevil education will be resolved in the current climate. The paradox of education is as troubling for parents as it is for teachers.

The Paradox for Parents and Students

Many parents feel rebuffed by a system that, on paper, attempts to reach out and involve them in the process. Across the country, schools are being told as never before to listen to parents and seek their advice, and many are drafting "improvement plans" in consultation with parents and others in the community. "Partnership" is the overworked word of the day, as education leaders attempt to demonstrate their willingness to move beyond the historic divide of "them" and "us" that separates parents and teachers. But in the experience of some parents, the paradox of education is that, in practice, the system is as resistant as ever to building real bridges to the outside world.

By any yardstick, Harold Lockhart, a Scarborough, Ontario, parent, embodies the definition of the traditional supporter of public education in Canada. He and his wife, Bonnie, take a strong, active interest in the education of their daughter, Jennifer, who graduates from high school this year. Lockhart pays public school taxes in three different jurisdictions, on his business, home and cottage, and says he would gladly pay more if the schools lived up to their side of the bargain.[2]

Instead, after years of frustrating skirmishes with teachers and principals, Lockhart is fed up with a system that made him feel like an outsider. "The school is like a fortress and no one can break into it," says Lockhart. In his experience, teachers were content to set low standards and expectations for their students and for themselves. Similarly, he felt school officials were bent on brushing problems under the carpet. As he puts it, "They sit there and they listen to you. But you know right away that they can't wait to get rid of you. They can tune you out."

Several years after the event, the Lockharts remain incensed by the local high school's reluctance to treat seriously their concerns about Jennifer's difficulties in math. Like many schools across Canada, her high school promotes the importance of math for all students, especially girls; for example, school posters exhort students to stick with math after Grade 10, when it is possible to drop the subject under Ontario curriculum guidelines. However, since math is the ticket to more than eighty jobs and a requirement for several programs in university, students drop the subject early at their peril, prematurely cutting off their options.

In spite of the school's official commitment to the importance of math, several of Jennifer's math teachers did their best to dissuade her from persevering in the subject. Since Jennifer had difficulties in Grade 10, the math teacher advised her to drop the subject at the end of the year. Instead, with strong encouragement from her parents, Jennifer took extra summer courses and worked with a $40-a-week tutor to conquer the subject.

Early in Grade 12, when Jennifer again was floundering, the Lockharts sought advice from her math teacher on parents' night. Once again, the immediate suggestion was that Jennifer should drop the subject. Harold Lockhart objected, pointing out that such a defeatist attitude ran counter to the school's stated commitment to setting high expectations for students. "I said, 'Under no circumstance is she going to drop math. I will get her a tutor. We will get her help. We will do everything you want.'" The teacher offered little encouragement and, ultimately, never followed through on a promise to recommend a tutor for Jennifer. In the end, worried about spending all year in class with a teacher unwilling to provide much support, Jennifer switched to another teacher who taught a less demanding math program. Delighted with her new teacher, Jennifer earned a B average that year.

For Jennifer's father, the troubling conclusion is that schools are quick with the politically correct platitudes of education such as "parental involvement" and "excellence," but seem reluctant to translate them into practice. "On one hand, the board of education is saying, 'We want the parents involved.' On the other hand, they are saying, 'If there is a problem, we don't want you involved.'"

Students themselves experience another paradox of education. Officially, every level of the education system, as well as the federal government, spends millions of dollars a year on programs and campaigns to make school an inviting, exciting experience for students. But for many, the day-to-day reality is one of boredom, indifference and low expectations. In its 1991 survey of school leavers, Statistics Canada found that three out of ten students who had ever left school cited boredom as the principal reason for leaving before graduation.[3]

Many of the students who stay the course often feel they are marking time. Just months away from graduating from a high school that boasts an academic reputation, Jennifer declares vehemently, "I can't wait to get out of this school. I don't think they are really concerned with the individual student." In her experience, teachers were happy to help students who naturally excelled in math, for example, and were less committed to students who struggled. "If you don't reach a certain grade point average, to them [the teachers] you have no business being in the school. You are just there to fill up space." Whether or not the teachers are less committed to some students, the perception of a double standard is there and thus cannot be ignored if schools expect to fulfil the promise of serving all members of the class.

The rumblings of dissatisfaction reverberate across Canada. From Newfoundland to British Columbia, grassroots groups of parents have sprung up in the past two years, demanding schools deliver more content, more structure and, above all, higher standards. In Ontario, parents queue up all night to enrol their children in publicly funded schools that stand out from the pack because of their commitment to academic rigour and discipline.

Some parents have turned away from public education altogether. In British Columbia, Alberta and Ontario, for example, fundamentalist religious schools are the fastest growing segment within private education, a response to parental objections to the loss of traditional teaching methods and the rise in incidents of violence in regular schools. In British Columbia, government funding for private schools jumped 13.2 per cent based on rising enrolment in 1991-92, compared to a rise of 3.2 per cent for the public system where student numbers grew more slowly.[4] For financial reasons, academic private schools are an option available only to a few. More often, parents quietly take matters into their own hands by investing hundreds of dollars a year in private tutoring and remedial reading and math programs. A growing cadre of private entrepreneurs sees a great opportunity to capitalize on the fear factor among parents who have lost confidence in schools.

By contrast, some parents have not lost faith in their schools. But they are by no means complacent and, like others, see the contradictions in education. One such parent is Heather Smith of Ottawa, the mother of two elementary school children, who is devoting her time and energy to develop a consensus about education in her community. On a regular basis, she and other parents meet with teachers, school administrators and others in education to discuss how to improve the level of discourse and lines of communication between the school and the community at large. "What we are caught up in now is a situation where education is such a huge bureaucracy," she says, citing the size of the public school board, the provincial ministry bureaucracy and the teachers' unions. "We are all institutionalized with power bases and vested interests and our own positions to protect. We can never look beyond that to what we as a society or we as a community need or what I as a parent want for my children and, therefore, for other children....What happens when you have these kinds of huge bureaucracies is that you get dehumanization, depersonalization, boredom. I hear administrators saying to me 'Parents don't want that kind of discussion. Nobody is going to come out and listen to that sort of stuff.'"

But Smith strongly disagrees with their attitude. "It's not so," she says. "Discussions need to be framed in terms that will interest them (parents)....We need to sit down and talk about what it is we want as an end result, and then we need to talk about how we are going to get there, and how that structure is to look. But the first step is more information. More people have to be involved in the discussions."

The message from parents is loud and clear. The education system must change so that parents and others in the community are heard in a more meaningful way. Without a change in both attitude and structure, the school system will continue to thwart parents and others from taking their share of responsibility for education.

The Paradox for Teachers

Classroom teachers and school principals, those on the front line of the battle over education, find a paradox in the situation much as parents do. Teachers complain that their voices are not heard in a system that, on the surface, promises consultation and involvement on issues affecting the quality of life for all students. Increasingly, teachers feel alienated in a system that expects them to be its chief advocates, especially to parents, for what happens in the classroom.

In a 1992 national study of Canadian teachers, their work and quality of life — the largest survey done to date — Queen's University researchers asked teachers whether they felt they had meaningful input into educational policy making. According to the survey, only 17 per cent of the 17,000 Canadian teachers surveyed felt they had a "meaningful dialogue with government"; the positive responses ranged from a high of 47 per cent in Prince Edward Island to a low of 14 per cent in Ontario.[5]

In the current politically charged atmosphere in education, teachers bear the brunt of criticism for mediocre student achievement even as they see budget cuts for support services eroding their ability to improve class performance. In Fredericton, New Brunswick, elementary school teacher Bonnie Carson sums up the frustration of many of her peers across Canada. "Provide me with the resources to teach the children," she declares. "At the moment I have no one to turn to when I have a discipline problem. I don't have the guidance counsellor, the social worker, the speech pathologist to deal with the special needs of integrated students [those with diagnosed emotional, physical and learning disabilities]." In a plea to education administrators, Carson begs, "Believe in me!" She says, "My professional opinion never seems to be good enough. If I try to go to the school board and say 'I need a teacher assistant,' they look at me as if I am looking for a free ride."

Like Carson, teachers across the country say they are exhausted from the pressures of performing a difficult balancing act. On the one hand, they strive to meet an ever-broadening range of students in the classroom. On the other, they find themselves responding to a proliferation of directives from school board and ministry bureaucracies. For example, in response to public pressure, school board trustees enunciate policy goals for schools to retain all their students and, at the same time, to maintain high standards.

The contradictions inherent in trying to meet the two goals simultaneously are rarely discussed by teachers, parents and school board trustees and, thus, they are never resolved to anyone's satisfaction. The classroom teacher is left to sort out the ambiguities on a day-to-day basis, pushing all students to work harder without losing any along the way. Reconciliation of such ambiguities is not only possible, but essential. However, it cannot be done by leaving the classroom teacher stranded without a lifeline.

Moreover, among many teachers, the mood is one of cynicism about the real intent of school reform. Even as they confront the reality of more students coming to school hungry and otherwise not ready to learn, teachers find themselves battling for support staff, books and other resources that are being slashed from school board and ministry budgets. As one weary Vancouver teacher sighed, "We are burned out. That is the long and the short of it."

Though school reform is crucial to rebuilding public confidence in education, it will be for nought without the active commitment and endorsement of teachers. Like parents, teachers must shoulder their share of the load for raising standards and expectations for students. Like parents, teachers must be part of a meaningful dialogue — beyond the current superficialities about consultation — to ensure greater responsibility and accountability for those in the classroom. However, the paradox of education will not be resolved until all the players agree to clear up the confusion that now surrounds complaints about school performance.

The Cause of Confusion

Canadians do not know how their schools are doing, and this lack of knowledge feeds public paranoia over the state of education. What few measures exist offer a limited and sometimes misleading portrait of a complex system.

One of the most blatant examples is the mythology and misunderstanding that surround the issue of student drop-outs. The most quoted figure on drop-outs, usually used to raise the alarm about declining education quality, is a national rate of 30 to 33 per cent estimated by Employment and Immigration Canada. Two points are rarely mentioned about the statistic, perhaps because they would blur a seemingly black and white picture of mediocrity. First, the drop-out rate has declined steadily over the past forty years. In Ontario alone the graduation rate of eighteen-year-olds has climbed dramatically since the mid-1950s.[6] In 1956, a mere 30 per cent of eighteen-year-olds received a high school diploma. By 1976, the figure had doubled to 61 per cent and a decade later rose again to 74 per cent. Second, the drop-out rate itself over-estimates the number of students who leave school, comparing those who graduate from high school to the number who entered Grade 9 four or five years earlier. As a gross number, the drop-out rate includes students who left one school for another; it does not acknowledge the "drop-in" phenomenon of students returning after an absence of a semester or more to earn their high school diploma.[7] The lack of co-operation among school districts and provinces in tracking students makes it difficult to develop a clear profile of drop-outs. However, Statistics Canada estimates that the net figure, on a national basis, is about 23 per cent.

The point here is not to whitewash the incidence of students who leave school prematurely. Even by Statistics Canada's yardstick, one in five students dropping out without a diploma suggests an unacceptable level of wastage in human terms and unconscionable inefficiency relative to the amount of public money spent on education. However, Canadians first must be well-informed about the state of education, based on reliable measures of performance. Otherwise, it will be impossible to have a thoughtful, and much needed, debate about where we stand now and where we must get to in the future.

The same risks of over-simplification occur in complaints about Canada's lacklustre performance on international comparisons of student achievement. In the most recent study, the 1992 International Assessment of Educational Progress (IAEP) examined a representative sample of students at the ages of nine and thirteen on their knowledge of mathematics and science.[8] Among thirteen-year-olds in mathematics, for example, Canada ranked ninth out of twenty countries, a showing seen as second rate, given that Canada spends more on education, relative to the gross national product (one measure of the country's total economic wealth), than almost any other industrial country. As a result, the IAEP data provided more ammunition for critics unhappy about the quality of education in Canada at a time when countries are competing on the basis on their knowledge skills.

However, the IAEP data also showed that at least 10 per cent of the students performed well (twenty points or more above the IAEP average) while another 10 per cent performed poorly (twenty points below the average). Again, as with the drop-out statistics, the point is not to sink back into complacency about student performance, but to acknowledge that some Canadian students are doing very well. The issue, then, is how to learn from those jurisdictions where students are high performers so that effective techniques in teaching and learning can be shared for the benefit of all students. In what few comparisons exist, student achievement rises in an east-to-west pattern, with students in the Maritimes, Québec and Ontario usually lagging behind those in Alberta and British Columbia. In its research, the Economic Council of Canada was unable to find an adequate explanation, citing the need for more research on effective schools. The plea for more and better research needs to be made again. In the absence of dependable data, interest groups of every stripe will use data selectively to further their own agenda to condemn or defend the system. Without adequate data and research, Canadians cannot make informed choices about education.

In the current climate, the public has lost patience with a system that produces only middling results — at a cost of $50.5 billion for education at all levels in 1991. (A figure of $34.4 billion for elementary and secondary schools accounts for the lion's share of the total.)[9] The IAEP results, coupled with such indicators as the 1989 Statistics Canada literacy survey that shows that 38 per cent of adults aged sixteen to sixty-nine "do not meet everyday reading demands" and a similarly large proportion lack everyday skills in numeracy,[10] amount to no less than a wake-up call for the country.

Like parents, employers are losing confidence in a system that fails to turn out graduates with the skills and attitudes needed to cope in a more uncertain, technology-based environment. In a 1992 speech, C.E. Ritchie, then chairman and chief executive officer of the Bank of Nova Scotia, acknowledged the strengths of the education system but warned that improvements are needed for Canada to survive in the future. "We may wring our hands over poor performance on international tests in science and mathematics," he observed, "[but] a closer look at the numbers shows that in the *early* grades Canadians are right up among the best. So there is nothing wrong with our raw material....Where we North Americans fail to do a good job is with the average performer. But it is precisely the education and training of the average performer that counts most in creating the broad base of skills for a modern competitive economy."[11]

Small business interests are no less worried about the capacity of education to deliver the goods. In a 1991 survey of its members, the Canadian Federation of Independent Business reported rising levels of dissatisfaction with the education and training institutions at all levels in preparing graduates for the workforce.[12] It is worth noting, however, that Canadian business has one of the poorest track records in its commitment to education and training, compared to other countries. Canadian industry spends 0.3 per cent of gross domestic product on training, less than half that of the United States and nearly eight times less than that of Germany.[13]

Adding to the muddled picture is the appearance of constant motion in education without conclusive signs of improvement. Almost every province, in response to public demands for accountability, has either pledged or is implementing curriculum and assessment reforms. Other measures, such as the introduction of junior kindergarten in most provinces, recognize that social and child-care programs contribute to young children being better prepared for the first year of school. At issue in some provinces is whether the ministry of education, other social agencies or the local school board should foot the bill for education programs with a strong social flavour. Shrinking government resources explain other kinds of reforms, such as Prince Edward Island's plan to wipe out local school boards. Meanwhile, school boards also talk the language of change, with new programs to define what students should achieve at key stages of elementary and secondary schools.

At first glance, the reform efforts seem to respond to public demands for a more accountable system with clear expectations of student achievement. In practice, the reforms fall short of the mark because they lack the specifics necessary for the public at large to assess what schools are doing or how well they do it. In overhauling its education system to put the learner at the centre of the education experience — a laudable objective — British Columbia fails to build in specifics that will reassure parents about the end result. For example, ministry documents refer to "learning experiences" for students, which begs the question of what knowledge and skills are essential for academic success. In other provinces, where similar efforts are underway to spell out expectations for student achievement, the exercise is bedevilled by the same lack of specificity.

The Absence of Consensus

Across the country, education is marked by turmoil and confusion. What expectations should Canadians set for their schools and for themselves? Canadians have long embraced the cult of "pretty good," demanding neither greatness nor excellence. Are we prepared, as a nation, to leave the sidelines and make sacrifices necessary to forge a new consensus on education? How can high expectations for education be met in an environment of scarce resources? Who controls the education agenda now and who should in future? Whose view prevails on any of these questions could set a new course for education.

However, public attitudes about education are increasingly polarized. Both supporters and critics of schools hold strong views, making it difficult at times to find common ground. Though the public is increasingly unhappy about the state of education, as the Angus Reid/Southam News poll indicates, 30 per cent of Canadians still believe that educational standards have improved over the past twenty-five years and 17 per cent sense no change at all. A similar split is evident in other surveys, which also highlight some of the contradictions in public attitudes to education. Although 56 per cent of those surveyed across the country by Gallup Canada in

September, 1992 expressed dissatisfaction with the education system, 69 per cent endorsed an increase in government funding for elementary and secondary schools.[14] In its 1992 poll on education in the province, the Ontario Institute for Studies in Education found that, despite the often-heard complaints about teachers, 73 per cent of those surveyed said school boards should not cut down on the number of teachers.[15]

The seeming contradictions and ambiguities in attitudes about education reflect, in large measure, the public's confusion about the claims and counterclaims made by interest groups on all sides about the nature and purpose of school. Business trumpets education as a tool of economic renewal for the country. Organized labour, including teachers' unions, recoils at regarding the school experience as a preparation for students to be tomorrow's workers. Taxpayer revolt groups rail at the rising cost of education while others contend, correctly, that spending on education, relative to other social services, is declining. Nascent grassroots parents' groups clamour for a stronger focus on the fundamentals of reading, writing and math, as well as a return to rote learning and teacher-directed instruction. However, education officials contend that new approaches to teaching and learning are essential to solving deep-rooted problems of school drop-outs and illiteracy.

Over the past year, a number of national organizations have attempted to draft goals for education, in hopes of producing a stronger consensus about education. The Canadian School Boards Association, which represents trustees, the Corporate-Higher Education Forum, which represents Canadian business executives and university presidents, and the Council of Ministers of Education, which represents the ten provinces and two territories, all took a run at drafting their own statement of goals. Although well intentioned, they all suffer from a lack of context, with no political imperative to pursue the goals in ways which hold anyone accountable for reaching them.

What explains the absence of consensus? The social contract that historically governed public education is breaking down for several reasons. Traditional institutions, such as the church and the family, have cracked beyond repair, leaving education to fill the gaps as a second-best solution. In attempting to be all things to all people — a substitute parent, moral teacher, social worker and baby sitter — schools often wind up satisfying no one. Unable to fulfil its academic goals or meet its social or moral mandate, the school winds up being blamed from all sides and thanked by no one. Nevertheless, education must heed the public unhappiness over the blurred mandate of schools or risk deeper political alienation on the part of those expected to fund public education.

The Risks of No Consensus

The unresolved arguments threaten the survival of public education. One risk is that those who can afford to walk away from the public schools will do so, further fragmenting society along class and religious lines. The danger in such a trend is that "separate but equal" institutions serve their own ethnic, religious or racial group, without ever having to rub shoulders with one another. At the moment, public schools are a crucible for Canadian society, spanning the cultural, racial, linguistic and economic diversity of the country. At this point, education is the only institution in the country that can provide the "glue" of shared values and history, providing its citizens with a sense of what it means to be a Canadian. In the absence of a continuing, strong commitment to public education in Canada, those who cannot afford the alternatives will be left to struggle with an already burdened system. As a result, Canada could wind up with a two-tier education system that further exacerbates political, social and economic divisions in the country.

Parents are a minority voice in contrast to the total number of Canadians who pay for the school system. Accordingly, a second risk is that those who have no children in public school will become even more restive about financing what looks like a bloated system. In the current environment, the greatest enemy for education is public cynicism that the system cannot or will not pull up its socks. Even as education authorities pledge change, the system is weighed down by institutional inertia and budget constraints that limit the scope of a transformation from within.

The fight over standards and assessment is only one of many that could redefine the education agenda in the 1990s. Trust is one of the missing links in education. In Ontario, where public anger over education runs high, even when the ministry undertakes an effort at evaluation, parents fault education bureaucrats for their reluctance to "come clean" with the public. Scarborough parent David Hogg, a member of the Organization for Quality Education, participated in an Ontario ministry review of student performance in math at the senior elementary grades in 1991. To his dismay, the terms of reference for the review panel allowed for subjective interpretation of the math results, allowing ministry bureaucrats to publish an overly rosy assessment of student performance. He and other dissident parents want the province to reinstate standardized testing of students at all grades, so that bureaucrats and teachers cannot manipulate the results.

How can the competing ideologies of back-to-basics and child-centred learning (in contrast to teacher-directed instruction) reconcile their differences so as to meet the demands of students for a rich and rigorous educational experience? Does the education system have the flexibility to deliver high standards without driving marginal students from the system? In testing for the new attributes of creativity, decision-making ability and entrepreneurship, will education deliver on its promise to teach the fundamentals?

Settling the heated conflict over spelling and reading, no less passionate than that on testing, represents another confidence test for education. The pendulum swings of reforms over the past thirty years, between the extremes of freedom and discipline, leave parents mistrustful that the current promises of innovation will only produce another cycle of fads.

Getting There from Here

To date, education reforms in Canada fall into one of two broad categories: to repair or to rebuild the system. Like the family car, education goes in for occasional tune-ups — the typical pattern of modification to Canada's schools. New courses on the environment and global education, computers in the classroom and co-op education all represent add-ons to the existing structure. Separately, the individual additions may make a lot of sense but taken together they provide no clear, well-articulated rationale of the educational experience intended for the student. In Ontario, for example, the governments of three different political parties tried over the past decade to make repairs to curriculum and testing policy. One government introduced measures only to have them undone in part by the next administration. The result, not surprisingly, is a hodge-podge of measures that leave the public understandably baffled as to the purpose. Given that history, it is not surprising that the New Democratic government's current efforts at reform, a re-working of ideas from the previous Liberal administration, have encountered strong resistance from sceptical school boards, teachers, parents and employers.

Like attempts at repairs, efforts to rebuild education are orchestrated centrally, by politicians and ministry bureaucrats. Like a mechanic who rebuilds a car engine in order to put the vehicle back on the road, education ministers introduce occasional, system-wide changes to revamp the system. In November 1990, Alberta's education minister, James Dinning, announced thirteen "priority directions" for the system to deliver excellence for all students. These included raising education standards, improving opportunities for native and immigrant children and encouraging school-community partnerships — all without additional spending on education. One year later, in an update on the system, he concluded, "Alberta has a good education system and a solid foundation to build on." The proposed reforms are to be implemented assuming no change in the fundamental structure of education decision making and finance in the province.

Like Alberta, New Brunswick is also rebuilding, though under the close supervision of Premier Frank McKenna. In September 1992, acting on a report by an independent inquiry staffed by two close allies, the premier pledged to spend $61.1 million on his "vision for excellence." Alone among Canada's premiers in his personal commitment to education, save for recent soundings from Ontario's Bob Rae, McKenna sees a healthier school system as his province's ticket to greater prosperity and social well-being. On education reforms, he moved with lightning speed to tighten central control; slash in half the number of school boards; spend more on early childhood education, provincial testing and the core curriculum; and require more days of actual schooling. Though it is too early to gauge the impact of the McKenna measures, they are significant already for sending a strong political message from the top about expectations and standards.

Finally, British Columbia has practised another type of re-building. While keeping the curriculum broadly intact, the pro-vince is reorienting the system to focus on the individual learner. To do so, the province is introducing significant changes to the way material is taught and learned, reminiscent of the revolutionary Hall-Dennis report on education in Ontario in the 1960s. British Columbia's approach puts more emphasis on helping students learn how to think analytically and creatively, skills now demanded by employers.

Repairs and rebuilding have their place, but in neither case is there any attempt to question fundamental assumptions about edu-cation. Yet the time has come to challenge traditional ideas about the structure and delivery of education in Canada. The eroding social contract for education, the speed of technological change and the extent of economic uncertainties are all requiring the school sys-tem to adjust more rapidly than ever before. At the same time, the fiscal pressure on education will force governments and the public to make difficult choices about scarce resources. Given these devel-opments, education cannot afford to take a business-as-usual approach to finance, governance, teacher education, curriculum or testing. Continuing the car analogy, it may be time to think about new models or even to ask if the car is the most appropriate vehicle for reaching one's destination. It is time, we believe, to reinvent edu-cation in Canada.

The precedent for reinventing education already exists. Corporate giants like IBM have been forced to trim their workforce, sharpen their focus and listen to their customers — or go out of business. Non-profit organizations, as well, have been forced to examine themselves, redefine their missions or reorganize to oper-ate more effectively. In its own way, the education community faces the same challenge to restructure itself or collapse from its own weight. Like these other bureaucracies, schools today operate in circumstances far different from those in effect thirty years ago.

Some innovative leaders in schools and communities across the country are already reinventing education to forge meaningful partnerships that deliver results. Indeed, the essence of reinvention is to make what happens in extraordinary schools the norm across Canada.

In reinventing education, Canadians will have an opportunity to rethink their attitudes, goals and expectations for schools in an era when dollars are tight. But in turning the system on its head, parents and other consumers have a chance to assert their rightful place in school affairs too long abandoned to the bureaucracy. A reinvigorated, consumer-oriented system would give those who use and pay for education a stronger political voice in the process — with more rights and more responsibilities.

The Politics of Solutions

There are no quick fixes. Solutions, when arrived at, will be labour-intensive. A more responsive system will demand more time, effort and sacrifice from all players in education. That is the price of success. Schools must be seen in a new light, as neither the fiefdom of the professionals nor the exclusive sphere of parents or employers. Education has to become a shared enterprise that involves students, parents, teachers and officials. "There is no question about sharing ownership of the issue," says Harvey Weiner, deputy secretary general of the Canadian Teachers' Federation. "Quite frankly, teachers are sick and tired of being blamed for all the ills of society." But he concedes that the professionals who have been used to managing the system on their own terms will have to relinquish some power in favour of those, such as parents, who now feel disenfranchised. He says the traditional response of teachers and education experts to say "We are the educators and we know what works best" is inconsistent with a political imperative to rethink the assumptions about education.

For public education to prosper in the future, bolder approaches are needed now. The current debate suffers from being mired in the politics of blame. Too often, one interest group skewers another for the real and perceived failings of schools. The exercise produces more heat than light, leaving education as someone else's problem to fix. Schools neither warrant nor deserve all the blame for academic and other shortcomings of students. Parents and employers must shoulder their share of the load if they want to strike a new deal with schools. If Canadians do take charge of their schools, they could have a system that ranks with the best in the world. To do so, they must look to the politics of solutions. "Every stakeholder has to be prepared to give up something and be able to commit to what's really important," declares parent Heather Smith, determined to work with school officials and others to build consensus in her community. "I don't think we have reached that point yet."

Neither education authorities nor the public can afford to waste time and money on exercises that create the appearance of reform without fundamental changes in the status quo. At each level — local, provincial and national — the public should know what schools and the system really stand for, and why. This does not now happen because there are no commonly agreed standards across or even within most jurisdictions.

Three principles should underpin efforts to win back public support for schools. The first is clarity, so that those inside and outside the system can work from an agreed set of goals. The second principle is integrity, so that the goals are worthwhile, achievable and measurable. Lofty commitments such as achieving a zero drop-out rate are meaningless if they float without targets and time-tables for implementation and execution. Politicians are quick to promise educational "excellence" and "equity," high standards and educational opportunities for all students, glossing over the contradictions that must be addressed to achieve both. The third principle is that students, teachers and schools hold themselves accountable for results — with the support of parents and the community at large.

Clarity, integrity and accountability must become the new touchstones for education, so that students and schools are seen to be making progress. These three principles are rarely present in the education picture today. Instead, many education insiders, such as teachers and bureaucrats, suffer from a siege mentality that assumes they can wait out the storm of protest beyond the school gates. Such an attitude is unproductive, feeding a sense of isolation and paranoia. Equally, parents and employers cannot afford to throw up their hands in despair at ever scaling the walls of the "fortress."

The politics of solutions looks for "what works," putting all the issues of teaching, learning and school decision making on the table for discussion. In the present climate, the debate on education is defined by sporadic outbursts between ideological antagonists over children who cannot spell or do their multiplication tables. Even then, the discussion is not among equals because the educational bureaucracy has more political clout than individual consumers, such as parents or employers.

Canadians need to raise their voices about education, turning that sound into deliberate action. It is time to rethink who really controls education and why. It is time to re-examine how the component parts relate to one another — and how they can be made to work better. It is time to probe what makes the system deaf to the voices of discontent within and beyond the fortress of education. It is time to reinvent education, in ways that make students, parents, teachers, taxpayers and employers responsible for results. The politics of solutions requires both a new national resolve and a commitment to local initiatives in education. Reinventing education is based on solutions that meet the test of clarity, integrity and accountability.

The choices in education are still open to Canadians. If parents, employers and taxpayers expect schools to perform their academic role, then schools must be redesigned to meet the social needs of students in other ways. Alternatively, if schools are to provide a range of academic and social services — a more likely scenario, given the squeeze on budgets — then schools must be given the necessary support and be held accountable for the results. At present, the lines of responsibility and accountability are blurred, creating frustration all around.

This book proposes a new dialogue for education reform. As such, the focus is not on sinners and saints but on solutions. We do not pretend to have the only blueprint for education reform. Rather, we hope to provoke new lines of inquiry and alternative approaches that will enable Canadians to feel good, with sound justification, about the money they spend on education. There is no single solution, no pat answer to the complex demands and expectations that surround the school system. In the end, we hope, Canadians will care enough about education to strike a new deal for their schools.

Chapter 2

Education
Under Stress

*E*very generation complains about the quality of education. But there is an extra edge to the criticisms in the 1990s. As consumers of education, students, parents and employers complain that the educational establishment does not listen to them. Classroom teachers say they, too, feel powerless in a system that ignores their concerns. Curiously, for all the consultation about the state of schools, there is a widely shared frustration that the exercise is an elaborate cover for bureaucratic or political inaction. In all quarters of the country, Canadians are beginning to ask why education is not delivering the goods.

What is going wrong? There are myriad explanations but what runs through them all is one central fact: *Canadian education is under stress.* When biologists apply that term to a living organism, they mean that its external environment is changing faster than its internal workings can adapt. The adaptability of all organisms to changing external conditions is vital to their survival. A human being, for example, can adjust readily to temperature changes within a limited range. For most of us, -40 to +40 degrees Celsius represents a tolerable range of temperature. People adapt to the normal changes in seasonal temperature by burning more energy in order to get warm or by sweating to cool off. These internal adaptive mechanisms enable us to withstand small variations in external temperature. Beyond the normal range, such as when experiencing an extraordinary drop in temperature, a person's ability to adapt breaks down and the body goes into shock. Under such stress, the body's internal organs cannot cope, and, with prolonged exposure to extreme cold, the person eventually dies.

The same is true of education. As long as the levels of public discomfort with the system are within their normal limits, the relatively slow-responding adaptive mechanisms in ministries and boards of education are adequate to keep up with the changes required. Usually, that is enough. But now, faced with rising public expectations for results, shrinking government revenues, shifting demographics and escalating social problems, the education system is not capable of making the kinds of speedy, sweeping adjustments demanded of it.

As every schoolchild knows, the lesson of the dinosaurs is that, over time, new species better adapted to their environment have evolved while their predecessors have become extinct. Some forecasters already predict the same fate for education. U.S. author Lewis Perelman, in a recent, damning critique of schools, mocks the current round of American reforms.[1] He argues that schools as we know them are obsolete and, in their place, we should adopt an entirely new approach to induce learning. In his view, educational reform in the 1990s is as pointless as improvements in buggy engineering and horse breeding would have been in the 1890s as a response to the invention of the motor car.

We disagree. As a social and political enterprise of society's own making, the school system is susceptible to reform if Canadians decide to take on the challenge. The thesis of our book is that educational reform is both possible and desirable. However, bringing about significant improvements in the way schools work will take a greater level of commitment and participation than Canadians have ever shown before.

Taking responsibility for Canada's schools requires that educational reform no longer be the exclusive domain of those who currently hold, and sometimes manipulate, the agenda for schools. Those used to running the system, be they ministry bureaucrats or school board administrators, trumpet the arrival of change and reform even as they cling to the traditional power structure. The educational establishment shows little enthusiasm for loosening the reins of power. By seizing the agenda from the insiders who treat the school system like a closed shop, those who use and consume the service — students, parents, taxpayers and employers — can participate fully in the reform exercise. By making informed choices about education, Canadians truly can create fresh opportunities to improve the future for their children and for the country. Taking responsibility for schools requires "ordinary Canadians" to learn more about how the education system works, to sort out the sensible from the silly in the diversity of voices and, most important, to invest more of their time and energy in building a better system.

"How will this help an education system under stress?" one may well ask. Just like the the organism under stress, the education system is not adapting to external upheavals; it has grown an almost airtight, watertight skin. Public education is slowly suffocating from an inability of the system to breathe. Inside the "skin" of education live ministry of education and school board officials, teachers and other providers of educational services. The outsiders are students, parents, employers and other members of the wider community who have only restricted access to the flow of ideas and information generated by the insiders. As such, the outsiders are limited to viewing the educational problems without having real influence on the solutions. There are few forums for a genuine exchange of ideas because the agenda for change is controlled from within the system itself. Is it any wonder that change is either resisted entirely or adjusted to suit those in command of the system? At no point do the insiders ask fundamental questions that might challenge the status quo.

Meanwhile, outside the education fortress, the level of frustration grows among parents, employers and others in the community who feel the system is unresponsive to their concerns. The response of those whose frustration has reached boiling point is to attack the system. As the *intifada* has shown in the Middle East, those who feel disenfranchised resort to throwing stones at those seen as in control. Here in Canada, the "stones" being thrown at our schools take the form of letters to the editor, speeches to business colleagues, appeals to members of parliament and the creation of ginger groups to press for reform.

These actions constitute the politics of blame. When all else fails, there is a feeling that one can at least find scapegoats for the shortcomings in Canada's schools. The last few years have seen a significant increase in educational protests by Canadians who, despite their best efforts, have been powerless to effect change. As in the Middle East, stone throwing may draw attention to the situation; it will not resolve it. Blaming the education system may provide short-term emotional relief. But it will not fix the problem. The time has come, we believe, to move beyond the politics of blame and on to the politics of solutions.

For Canadians, the first task in the politics of solutions is to understand how the external environment of education has changed and why its internal mechanisms prevent the necessary adaptation. An appreciation for the external environment of education and the internal workings of the system provides the basis to deliberate about the future of Canada's schools. Such a discussion not only must include all segments of society but must be held at every level — the school, the province and the country as a whole. By suggesting an agenda for deliberation about change in our education systems, we hope to provoke Canadians to participate in the difficult but ultimately rewarding exercise of building a significant consensus on education.

The Changing External Environment of Education

Canadians are only too aware of how uncertain their world is and how the rapid pace of change seems to be the one constant. For many Canadians, their communities have been transformed during the past decade by a diverse group of immigrants who bring their own cultures, languages and politics. For an increasing number of Canadians, the jobs on which they once counted for lifetime employment either offer no security or have disappeared altogether. Meanwhile, voices once heard only at the margin of society or not at all now demand their rightful place at the table, producing a cacophony of political, social and economic demands.

Much has been written on the forces of the Constitution, free trade, the redefinition of the family, the role of women in the workforce, new immigration patterns and the rise of minority rights, which have transformed the social, economic and political landscape of Canada. Collectively, these forces have had an enormous influence in modifying the goals and purpose of school and, not coincidentally, in altering the perception of Canadians about the quality of the education system. One cannot appreciate why education is a system under stress, or weigh possible solutions, without first examining the changing social, economic and political context of education.

The New Social Context

The face of Canada is changing in dramatic ways. According to the 1991 census, almost 15 per cent of the entire population of 27 million people speak neither English nor French as their mother tongue, a reflection of non-traditional immigration patterns to Canada over the past decade. The impact is felt most in Canada's largest cities. The United Nations recognizes Toronto, for example, as the most culturally and ethnically diverse city in the world. For some school and community meetings, translators are required to work in one or more of the fifty languages acknowledged by the Toronto Board of Education. When school trustees attend community meetings, they now speak in short sentences and pause until volunteer translators communicate the message to their language group! In response to the demands of an increasingly multicultural, multi-ethnic population, the board offers thirty-seven "heritage languages" in after-school programs.

Metro Toronto, which includes Toronto and area schools, received more than 60 per cent of new immigrants to Canada in 1991, 97 per cent of whom were unable to speak, read or write English.[2] Between 1980 and 1990, the proportion of students in Metro Toronto who spoke neither English nor French as their first language more than doubled to 45 per cent. The increase represents a sudden shock to the system, requiring extra teachers and other support services. According to research by the Toronto board, students who speak neither English nor French need an extra four to six years of language instruction to gain the proficiency needed to succeed in school.

Federal immigration policies have had enormous repercussions on the classroom. It is in the schools that the richness — and latent tensions — of the new ethnic and racial diversity of the country have their greatest impact. As the one institution in society where all these groups meet, school becomes an important vehicle for teaching tolerance and other shared values. Identifying and communicating those values, however, become more difficult as schools attempt to recognize and respect differences in religion and culture. On top of this, teachers who used to assume that they shared common life experiences with students in the classroom now find more differences than similarities. As a result, teachers have to find new approaches to involve and motivate students. It is not surprising, therefore, that white supremacists have targeted some Toronto and area schools in hopes of inciting racial tensions.

Parents in some minority groups complain that the traditional, Euro-centred curriculum is not relevant to their children. Nova Scotian blacks, whose roots in Canada extend back to the country's earliest days, are lobbying for changes to the school curriculum to recognize their place in history and in contemporary society. Caribbean-Canadian parents in Toronto received a political boost for their complaints about the system's treatment of their children when Stephen Lewis tabled his report to the Ontario government on the causes of the Toronto Yonge Street riot in early 1992. His report contained a scathing indictment of the failure of schools to address the needs of blacks. "It's as if virtually nothing has changed for visible minority kids in the school system over the last ten years," he wrote. "The lack of real progress is shocking." While acknowledging the "Herculean" effort of the Toronto board, Mr. Lewis concluded that the absence of progress "raises searching questions for communications and accountability."[3] Even as budgets shrink, schools are under pressure to hire more minority teachers who would also serve as role models for alienated youth. Ontario's New Democratic government is asking university faculties of education to set admission quotas for visible minorities, a request that immediately triggers questions about the trade-off between affirmative action and traditional indicators of merit.

As a mirror of society, the education system struggles to cope with other social challenges beyond its control. The proportion of single-parent families in Canada has risen by 130 per cent over the past twenty years.[4] One in six children in Canada lives in poverty, spurring schools to run hot breakfast and lunch programs for inner-city youth. Acts of random violence in school, between students or between students and teachers are on the rise, according to limited surveys by teacher organizations.

North York principal Hugh Beattie, a thirty-year veteran of the school system, is deeply troubled by the rising incidence of social problems in the school. "I have had more cases of sexual assault, kid to kid, in the last six months than I have had in the rest of my career," he said in 1992. Citing an array of behavioural problems now faced on a daily basis, he observed, "I am dealing more and more with that rather than curriculum issues."

The social consequences of two-income parents, single parents, latch-key children and an unstable student population (with parents moving in and out of the school district) all take their toll on the schools. In the absence of other institutions, schools bear a growing responsibility to serve as the social safety net for students in need. "We've become an all-purpose social service agency," observes one education official. As a result, he says, schools "can't deliver the goods." Schools are blamed for declining academic standards even as they attempt to deal with family problems that inhibit a student's ability to learn. "It's a lose-lose situation," says the official. The public loses because of the loss of academic focus in schools. Teachers lose because they sound defensive when trying to explain the forces beyond the school gate that erode standards and student achievement.

Schools cannot be expected to educate young people if they are sidetracked from their job of teaching and learning. Several provinces are exploring ways for education and other social services to collaborate more effectively, for less money, using schools as the focal point for youth services. In Ontario, the Premier's Council on Health, Well-Being and Social Justice has sponsored pilot projects to test the thesis. In this new fiscal environment, the competition for scarce public dollars will grow more intense, and education, health and related services will have to become more innovative in sharing the wealth. In its education reforms in 1992, New Brunswick recognized the role of health and community services in preparing young children for school, earmarking an extra $17.5 million over four years for preventive health measures. The choices are still ours to make; if schools are to carry out their academic role in full, they cannot be expected to deliver an array of youth social services on their own.

The Changing Economic Context

Many Canadian parents and employers are worried that today's students will be ill-prepared for tomorrow's jobs. They want assurances that students will get the basic knowledge and skills they need. One example of the shift taking place in the workplace is in the area of technology. In 1990, the Economic Council of Canada estimated that more than half of Canadians are now employed in jobs that rely on data and knowledge, accounting for two-thirds of net employment growth in the country between 1971 and 1986.[5] Yet advances in technology also polarize the job market, by creating a demand for both low-skilled workers in data processing and highly-skilled professionals with sophisticated knowledge and skills.

The effects of global competition, spurring firms to produce more with fewer workers, cut a wide swath across the economy as old-line car makers and the once-mighty banks permanently reduce their workforce. In the wake of the 1991-92 recession, employment for low-skilled workers declined while some highly skilled jobs could not be filled. These trends signal that economic divisions between "haves" and "have nots" on the basis on education will likely worsen in the years ahead. For young people starting out in the job market, the pay-off for staying in school — assuming they can find a job — is high. Among young people fifteen to twenty years old who do not complete elementary school, the unemployment rate is 30 per cent, according to Employment and Immigration Canada. However, for the same age group with some post-secondary schooling, the jobless rate is 13 per cent. The effect of these economic trends is to make parents more determined to see their children receive the best possible education.

Since the math and science component of the new value-added jobs is so important, parents are all the more alarmed when it appears that their children are not learning the basics. What's worse, fewer than one-quarter of senior high school students take math and science, and university enrolment in these critical subjects continues to drop.[6]

Given the economic trends, public expectations for education continue to escalate. On a positive note, more students are graduating than twenty years ago, and more student drop-outs are returning to high school to earn their diploma. Nevertheless, Canada's record is dismal compared to the record in Germany and Japan, two of the world's economic leaders. Jim Bennett, vice-president and general manager of the Canadian Federation of Independent Business, which represents 80,000 small businesses across the country, says schools must do a better job to meet rising public expectations. In his view, it is "not good enough" that more students are completing school. The issue, Bennett contends, is that too many students leave school prematurely and those who graduate lack the necessary work ethic, knowledge and skills.

As Canadians close the door on the twentieth century — which was to have been Canada's according to one bold prediction 100 years ago — they see a new global economic order challenging the traditional assumptions on which Canada's high standard of living has been based. Historically, while Canada has prospered selling its natural resources to the world, less resource-rich countries in Asia have used their brain power to forge a competitive edge. Canada's heavy reliance on resources, in a global marketplace that rewards the "intelligence" component of value-added products, increasingly is called into question. For years, Canadians have been urged to shift economic gears to produce more value-added jobs in Canada. In its two-year consultation on the economy and education, the federal government's "prosperity" task force again called for Canadians to become more innovative and competitive. In its report, *Prosperity Through Innovation,* the Task Force on Challenges in Science, Technology and Related Skills concludes:

> For Canada, the decisions required to successfully adapt to the reality of globalization do not involve favoring one sector over another, as much as they are concerned with how innovation is used to strategic advantage. And while natural resources will

continue to play an important role in the Canadian economy, the success of resource-based industries will be inextricably linked to the development of people and the application of technology .... The future of our manufacturing industries ... will depend on successful innovation through the application of technology and the development of people.[7]

The message is not new. Like countless earlier reports, the federal task force called for an "innovation-based" economy that values science, technology and an effective education system. "Canadians must learn to live by their wits," concludes Janet Halliwell, chair of the technology task force. However worthy the sentiment, the current imbalances in the economy underscore the difficulty in making the transition to an economy built on the brain power of its people. At present, Northern Telecom, a Canadian multinational built on its close ties to Bell Canada, performs one-quarter of all industrial research and development in Canada.[8] Moreover, Canadian firms lag well behind other countries in the education and training of their workers, and the country is ranked nineteenth out of twenty-two industrial countries, according to the 1992 World Competitiveness Report.[9]

Public uncertainty about the future shape and direction of the economy creates rising expectations for the education system. Though the links between a healthy economy and the school system are by no means clear-cut, neither the education sector nor the public can ignore the impact of global competitiveness on a local community's job market. For that reason, the corporate sector in Canada is one of the new players trying to shape the agenda for schools. They do so in a climate of mistrust about motives on all sides. On one hand, business is not convinced that schools are turning out flexible graduates able to communicate, think and continue to learn.[10] Moreover, like other members of the public, business wants clearer measures of performance in education. On the other hand, many teachers and education officials are suspicious that business has a so-called "corporate agenda," which seeks to use the education system as a vehicle for producing pliable, trained workers. Keith Gray, a vice-president of the British Columbia Council of Business, concedes, "There's a lack of trust." Business, he says, must play a larger role in helping schools to do their job better. "I can assure you that the business community knows it cannot run schools, just as teachers know they couldn't run a corporation."

The Changing Political Context

Education is not only a social and economic undertaking; it involves an intensely political struggle over choices. The debate in Canada extends to all facets of life at school, including what is taught and how it is taught. In British Columbia and Ontario, proposed curriculum changes are designed to turn out graduates who are flexible and creative thinkers. But the new direction, with its focus on process (learning how to think) rather than content (learning what to know), is controversial. While supporters of the curriculum reforms argue that students will learn how to do research and think for themselves, critics say the pendulum has swung too far away from teaching students a core body of knowledge.

The level of public mistrust over the reforms underscores a new dimension to the debate over education in the 1990s. The 1982 Charter of Rights and Freedoms gives individuals and groups a new political tool for asserting their rights, such as the demand for minority language school boards in many provinces. The public's repudiation of the constitutional compromise in October 1992 is only one recent demonstration of frustration with the country's élites. The population is growing increasingly intolerant of politicians at all levels of government and the level of taxation required to pay for public services.

The same trend is evident in education. In 1992, Scarborough, Ontario, taxpayers revolted when public school board trustees voted themselves a 64 per cent pay raise in the midst of a recession. Several months later, the trustees rolled back a portion of the increase, still giving each trustee a salary of $30,000 a year. The Scarborough incident, notable for the trustees' reluctance to heed the taxpayers' message, has sparked calls from some taxpayers for an elimination of some school boards. Metro Catholic trustees also incurred taxpayer wrath by voting themselves funds to attend a winter conference in California. Faced with angry protests, the trustees rescinded the decision in January 1993.

Piqued by the political insensitivity of school trustees, some taxpayers are beginning to question the role of boards of education. With so many political layers and bureaucracy, the public is confused about what they do. Now, in tight fiscal times, the public is asking whether they are needed at all. Metro Toronto, with one of the most top-heavy political bureaucracies in the country, has 112 trustees and nine different publicly funded boards for almost 380,000 students. Some countries, such as Britain and New Zealand, have moved to disband school boards. In Canada, New Brunswick and Prince Edward Island have reduced the number of trustees, largely for budgetary reasons.

The new political context for education is also being shaped by fiscal and demographic realities. As the population ages, a greater proportion of public expenditures will shift away from education to health and pensions, as indicated by research by the C.D. Howe

Institute.[11] In other words, educational institutions are only beginning to feel the pinch. The fiscal pressures will undoubtedly highlight some of the "sacred cows," such as pensions and benefits for teachers, the layers of senior management in school boards and ministries and the use of board consultants.

Like industry, public institutions need to lose weight. Education cannot escape the painful exercise of downsizing and restructuring underway at such corporate giants as IBM and General Motors. For the past fifty years, education has been highly regulated by a vast army of bureaucrats at provincial, regional and local levels of government. Such a structure is unsustainable given the budgetary and demographic imperatives of the 1990s.

A new approach, suggested in the provocative American book *Reinventing Government*, is for the public to rethink the basic role of government in society. The authors cite E.S. Savas, a professor at the City University of New York, who argues that governments should learn to "steer, not row the boat." In this role, governments would concentrate on setting the general policy direction, leaving others in society to sort out the means of getting there. As Savas puts it, "Delivering services is rowing, and government is not very good at rowing."[12] In education, the same principle applies as the two key layers of government — the provincial ministry and local school boards — try to set the policy course and implement it with extensive rules and regulations. The move to school-based decision making, for example, gives those on the front lines freedom to hire staff and spend money in ways that meet local needs but satisfy provincial goals.

Why Education Can't Adapt

Beset by external pressures — social, economic and political — that challenge the way things have been done in the past, the education system is remarkably resistant to change. It is the intractability of the system that so enrages those on the outside demanding improvements. Education encases itself in a protective layer or skin, insulating itself from outside influences. To understand how the system works (or, rather, fails to work), we must "get under the skin" of a complicated and bureaucratic system to answer the question "Who's in charge?"

Figure 1: Insiders and Outsiders in Education

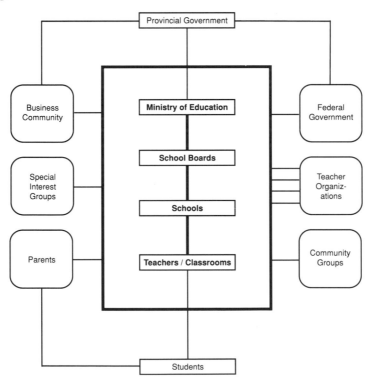

Figure 1 shows in highly simplified outline how the education system operates in all provinces. The diagram illustrates two important characteristics of all the systems. First, the "insiders" operate inside the confines of a clearly delineated structure. From ministry of education bureaucrats at the top, through school board officials in the middle, to school principals and teachers in the classroom, all have been socialized into the same mould. In order to gain access to the hierarchy, one needs a series of paper qualifications. One cannot move up the ladder without first gaining experience in the ranks below, often starting in the classroom. Moving up the hierarchy, in rank and pay, is tied to acquiring additional specialist qualifications. Such a gate-keeper model effectively cuts off "new blood" that might introduce radical ideas that threaten the status quo. There is no area of public life other than the military in which positions of policy making and regulatory authority are so totally dominated by professionals from the field. Change in this "edu-culture" is thus enormously hard to achieve, as ministers of education (nominally in charge, but effectively outside the system) have discovered to their dismay.

A second striking feature is that the insiders relate to each other, not to the outside public, according to a rigidly maintained hierarchy. The philosophy and agenda of education are set at the senior levels of ministries and boards, with those in the classroom expected to fall in line. It would be inappropriate, unprofessional and unwise for those lower in the ranks to challenge their superiors. New directions and ideas generated at the top are articulated in greater detail as one moves down the system, until classroom teachers convert the policies into reality. However, those on the lower rungs of the hierarchy have ways to confound this "factory model" of school organization. Professionals at each level of the system take the edicts from above with a pinch of salt. Once the classroom door is closed, for instance, teachers carry on with practices they perceive to be in the best interests of their students.

The third significant feature of the system is the place of outsiders, all those without actual decision-making authority over schools. They are grouped around the system, some with more effective lines into the hierarchy than others. The outsiders have a formal say at election time, for either a new government or new school trustees. But education tends not to rank high as a provincial election issue and voter turnout for school boards is notoriously poor. Beyond these influences, the linkages to the hierarchy are informal, with few forums for debate and deliberation between insiders and outsiders. Interventions at school board meetings usually are limited to groups and individuals petitioning on one side or another of a specific issue, making it difficult to raise more probing or wide-ranging questions about larger policies. Not surprisingly perhaps, the best connected outsiders are the teachers' unions, who know how to gain access to, and operate within, the bureaucratic hierarchy. After all, their members and former members are distributed throughout the system.

The workings of the system can best be traced by looking at an example, such as testing. Under successive governments since the late 1960s, the Ontario Ministry of Education has opposed a return to province-wide testing of students in their final year of high school. In the 1980s, in response to growing public demands for accountability, the ministry spent $10 million developing a package of test questions to measure student achievement. The questions were made available to school boards for use on a voluntary basis, which thus sidestepped a political confrontation with teacher groups opposed to testing and effectively ruled out comparisons on a provincial basis.

Some school boards used the package of questions to evaluate students in their jurisdiction. But by the late 1980s, the ministry quietly shelved the project to work on another student evaluation program, known as benchmarks. Given the ministry (and ministerial) reluctance to proceed with province-wide testing of all students, several large boards developed their own testing programs to respond to public demands for accountability. Since each board had a different philosophy on what should be tested, the public still cannot judge the performance of the system as a whole. Even among boards committed to regular evaluations of students, teachers and board officials are reluctant to publish the results in a way that allows for school-by-school comparisons.

Meanwhile, an increasing number of "outside" groups — parents, university admissions officers, business people, among others — are begging to find out more about how students are actually performing. The "edu-crats," however, safe within the walls of their fortress, decreed, "Testing if necessary, but not necessarily testing." The crisis of confidence that this issue alone has engendered has consumed at least one minister of education in Ontario and threatens the credibility of the entire system.

The six major reasons for the protection of the "fortress" are also the reasons the walls must come down. These six provide the framework for the major part of this book. Each reason for the education system's inability to adapt presents an opportunity for examining our assumptions and for reinventing the system.

1. Education is a rigid bureaucracy

Under the Constitution, each province has jurisdiction over education. Nevertheless, all the provincial systems are similar in structure, though the degree of centralized control over course guidelines, testing and funding of schools differs from one jurisdiction to another.

In every case, the system is bureaucratic and unresponsive to the user, largely because government is the sole institution responsible for setting the agenda for schools. Public education functions as the only game in town, with only limited competition from the private sector. Moreover, public schools provide few variations in teaching philosophy, making it difficult for parents to seek significantly different approaches to the education of their children. Though the society in which schools operate has changed fundamentally over the past twenty-five years, parents have few options to select schools that offer a truer reflection of their own values. Teachers and schools are at the bottom of the hierarchy and are expected to abide by policy directives and regulations drafted by ministries and school boards, with little voice in the decision-making process. Local schools are expected to adapt policies developed elsewhere to the specific needs of students, though there may be insufficient resources to do the job.

A re-examination of the current structure is overdue. A new structure could redistribute power, now concentrated at the ministry and school board level, in two different directions. First, power should be decentralized to the local level, so teachers and parents can have more authority to develop programs that meet the needs of their students. Second, some power should be centralized through a new co-operative effort to set agreed national standards for student achievement. The environmental slogan "Think globally...act locally" is apt for redesigning the structure of education. In a reinvented school system, the public would have a voice in setting educational standards at the national level for the first time. In this way, the terms of the education agenda would not be defined exclusively by provincial ministries and school boards. At the same time, parents, teachers and other members of the community would have a stronger voice in the affairs of their school — with heightened responsibilities for ensuring success for all students.

2. Schools are not designed to maximize learning

Learning must be re-established as the primary function of schools. While educational fads come and go, the industrial model of today's schools dates back over one hundred years. In that time, however, researchers have developed new theories about how children and young people learn, identifying factors that support effective teaching strategies in the classroom. But these new ideas are not easily incorporated into the current definition of school. Moreover, though we have at our disposal an arsenal of new information technologies to support the learning process, most schools have barely explored the possibilities. In most Canadian classrooms, even a telephone link to the outside world is regarded as a radical innovation.

Time still is the main organizing element in operating schools and measuring education. Contact hours between student and teacher or years of schooling, rather than competencies or academic accomplishments, are the typical units of measurement in education. The students in school today inhabit schools based on educational and management principles of the nineteenth century, yet are heading into the work world of the twenty-first century.

Another challenge to traditional thinking is to focus on the learner, usually treated as the least important person in education. The most interesting innovations now recognize students as the central players, so they gain more control over their academic lives. The *quid pro quo* is that students demonstrate that they have acquired the requisite skills and knowledge.

Schools must be encouraged to redefine themselves to help students make stronger links between their work in the classroom and the outside world. A similar dose of pragmatism is needed to address the controversy over teaching strategies. Since there is no single, successful method of instruction, schools should be encouraged to adopt practices and strategies — even the unconventional — so long as they demonstrate results for students.

3. Education lacks consensus on goals

Throughout the twentieth century, schools have always juggled competing goals. Students are expected to acquire core knowledge and skills, acceptable social habits, self-esteem and shared values and beliefs. Of late, however, the juggling act has become more perilous as the definition of each goal has broadened, upsetting the balance among them. Schools are burdened with conflicts over what knowledge and skills are worthwhile, disagreements about how to promote self-esteem and disputes over values and beliefs.

School responsibility for the intellectual growth of the student now includes teaching drug education, gender equity, anti-racism and tolerance for gay rights in a curriculum crammed with an array of new programs over the past decade. The school's role in promoting the social growth of the student now includes the provision of quasi-custodial services in junior kindergarten and hot breakfast and lunch programs for hungry children. While traditionally concerned with a student's sense of well-being, schools now focus on self-esteem as an end in itself, such as with new programs and support services for students in danger of leaving school prematurely. The student population covers the ethnic, racial and linguistic spectrum, with inevitable clashes over the school's responsibility to honour cultural and religious differences.

Schools have taken on new responsibilities in the wake of a decline in other social institutions — the family and the church. In the process, schools have left the impression they could meet these new social obligations and still turn out graduates equipped for life.

In reality, schools suffer from blurred vision, brought on by conflicting and as yet unresolved public demands. Until they clarify the primary purposes of education, schools and the public will be unable to raise standards and expectations for all students.

4. Education shows little concern for results

Parents, taxpayers and employers want reliable measures of how students and the system as a whole are performing. Bitter conflicts over what knowledge and skills should be assessed, and how they should be measured, underscore the deterioration in public trust of the educational "experts." In designing more sophisticated tools to measure a wider range of student achievement, teachers and other testing experts have ignored the public's desire for clarity, simplicity and comparability. Parents want a number or letter grade that will show where students stand in relation to the rest of the class. The public wants more comprehensive data that show whether all schools are improving, especially relative to Canada's global competitors.

The absence of national and provincial standards is a major weakness for Canada. Although most provinces test all students as they leave high school, cross-country comparisons of student performance, teaching practices and course content are almost nonexistent.

Sceptical about leaving teachers in charge of assessment, some parents and business groups want more external evaluations of students and the system as a whole. The most vociferous critics demand a return to old-fashioned external tests of the schools, a type of evaluation to which teachers object most strongly. The public interprets the teachers' resistance as opposition to any form of testing and a disregard for standards. The partisan war on testing has to end. Teachers and their critics must turn their considerable energies to devising tests that not only describe how students are doing but show where they need to improve.

5. Education is a priesthood

The education community speaks a foreign language best described as "eduspeak." Many of the terms used by education professionals make an unnecessary mystery of schooling: "child-centred learning" (teachers assist students to think for themselves, instead of directing instruction from the front of the class); "whole language" (a teaching approach to spelling and reading that encourages students to discover the meaning of words in context, with less emphasis on learning to read and spell phonetically); "continuous progress" (since students learn at different rates, schools are reluctant to fail students); "attention deficit syndrome" (students with learning or behavioural difficulties cannot concentrate). The buzz-words and jargon of education feed public suspicion that teachers and education officials have something to hide. An honest discussion of ideas and choices will not be possible until the education community — and the responsibility begins there — dismantles the language barrier.

The jargon is symptomatic of a larger problem: public mistrust of ideas and trends in education. The phenomenon of duelling ideologies among vested interests creates the impression that the education system feeds on fads, not facts. Citing data selectively to suit their ends, experts from across the political spectrum argue over the practice of grouping students by levels of ability, the merits of child-centred learning and teaching methods. Discussions of significant educational issues, such as testing and evaluation, are confined to spokespersons for particular interests, leaving the baffled public on the sidelines when they should be informed, engaged participants.

Schools must seek out parents and others as allies instead of enemies. Reshaping the structure, content and ethos of education depends on all groups recognizing their mutual interest in the success of schools. Without collective action, schools will not deliver results where they are needed most — in the classroom.

6. The education system does not renew itself

Unlike the United States, where the education debate has spawned hundreds of government and private-sector think-tanks over the past decade, Canada shows a dearth of research activity. Education is a $50.5-billion-a-year enterprise, yet the total research and development effort in Canada is minuscule in comparison. An investment in ideas is essential for reinventing education for the benefit of students and society at large.

Respect for teachers as professionals is a vital ingredient of renewing education. In return, teachers must show they will be accountable for what happens in the classroom. But they cannot do the job alone. University faculties of education and teachers' organizations should take a fresh look at teacher training, with an eye to the obstacles that slow the continuing improvement of good practice. The limited preparation time required to become a teacher — and the absence of regular exposure to the world outside the classroom — contribute to the professional isolation of teachers. Business, labour, higher education and government must contribute to giving teachers the tools they need to do a complex job well.

A New Deal for Education

Public education is a system under stress. Caught in a web of external changes not of their making, schools are trapped by rigid constraints that impede renewal of the system. However, the same factors that erode public confidence in education today also create the political conditions for striking a new deal for Canada's schools. Success depends on addressing the six issues outlined above. Dealing with some but not all of them is a recipe for failure; without consensus on goals, for example, the public cannot sort out what's worth learning. Without redistributing power, the local community cannot take full responsibility for its schools. Without a sharper focus on what we expect of students and schools, teachers will remain in their bunkers, trapped by the politics of blame. The price will be paid — as it is now — in missed opportunities for young people and rising cynicism among the public at large. However, an even heavier price will be exacted if Canadians and their educational institutions fail to seize the moment to reinvent schools along new lines.

Change has been a central theme of education over the past thirty years, though without a clear sense of forward momentum. Accordingly, any reform must meet the tests of clarity, integrity and accountability: schools must make clear what they are up to, deliver on the promise of quality programs and give the public reason to have confidence in the results. But schools cannot reform themselves alone — nor should they be expected to. Education is too vital to the country's well-being to be left to the experts or to the narrow agendas of particular interest groups.

With wit and energy, students, parents, taxpayers, employers, politicians and the education profession have a golden opportunity to revitalize schools in readiness for the next century. The exercise demands commitment over complacency, bridge building over brick throwing, ideas over money and inspiration over insularity. There is reason for optimism. The simple truth is that schools could do so much better — like Canadians themselves. We can no longer subscribe to the cult of "pretty good." Taking responsibility for Canada's schools is an overdue assignment.

Chapter 3

Redistributing Power

*I*n *1987, when* Malkin Dare of Waterloo, Ontario, went to the regular parent-teacher interview for a progress report on her Grade 2 son, she received a jolt. Armed with a "glowing" report received only one day earlier, Dare was told her son had reading difficulties. "He couldn't sound out words," she said. "If he was faced with an unfamiliar word, he couldn't read it." Dare and her husband already had been suspicious about their son's progress, but to that point were advised by the school to be positive, supportive and patient. Alarmed by her son's now-recognized difficulties, Dare questioned the school's use of new teaching techniques that replaced phonics, a traditional approach in which children sound out syllables as building blocks for creating words. In the end, Dare purchased her own phonics instruction books and taught her son to read.

Dare still bristles with indignation at the response of the local public school board to her concerns about the choice of teaching methods. "They just kind of dismissed me," she recalls. Although she succeeded in having a board committee convened to hear her complaints, Dare remembers the response from board representatives at the meeting as polite disinterest. A year later, Dare again appeared before the board, this time speaking for a newly minted parents' group lobbying for a return to phonics as the preferred way to teach children to spell and read. "Same story, even worse, really," she says. "There were one or two desultory questions. They said they would put it on the agenda and they never did. That was it. So it was worse. I guess they were ready for me this time."

Local Control

In raw terms, Dare's experience is an object lesson in power: who wields it, for whose benefit and to what ends. In public education, power traditionally rests with provincial ministries of education and school boards that essentially deliver a monopoly service. To the extent that alternatives exist, they are expensive (academic private schools), narrowly focused (private religious schools) or unsuited to the time demands on most families (home schooling). The educational professionals who provide the service (the "insiders" shown on Figure 1 of Chapter Two) not only have a lock on the service but on the criteria for judging the quality of the service as well. Students and parents who have the most immediate exposure to the education service have little choice in determining what is offered or how it is offered. In this sense, they are "outsiders" to a system that provides few natural forums in which their needs and concerns can be addressed. Home and school meetings typically are preoccupied with raising funds for school trips. School boards are engrossed with operational issues, leaving little opportunity for parents and others to participate except as petitioners on specific topics.

In 1991, Dare and other like-minded parents (and even some teachers) joined forces to form a grassroots reform movement known as the Organization for Quality Education (OQE), which now boasts twenty-six groups in Ontario and a small but growing network of educational dissidents across Canada. Dare estimates she spends about $4,000 a year and puts in between thirty and forty hours a week on what she ruefully describes as her charity. But underfinanced upstart protest groups such as OQE, with ideas that challenge the prevailing "progressive" philosophy in the education establishment, wage an uphill battle against entrenched bureaucracies and well-financed teacher lobbies.

Although she can chalk up some successes, Dare has learned through bitter experience how a powerful public bureaucracy can brush off the concerns of dissatisfied parents. "The first surprise was how defensive the education establishment was," she says, "and how they chose to take what I had to say as a personal attack....They tried to characterize me and others...as sort of red necks." Responsiveness to the client, especially one with a contrary point of view, is not characteristic of a monopoly service.

In public education across the country, bureaucrats and politicians at the provincial ministry and school board levels set the rules for schools; teachers and students live by them; and taxpayers pay the bill. These ground rules have governed the education sector for the past century. But in an environment marked by new external pressures and internal strains on the system, are the assumptions of the past adequate for the next century? For Dare and other disgruntled parents, taxpayers and employers, the answer is a resounding no! "If they stood to lose all their clients, they would stand up and listen," observes Dare of those who now manage public education.

Increasingly, the public is demanding a system of education that is more responsive, less arrogant and aloof. As consumers of a significant public service, parents and other members of the public feel shut out of a system that ignores their hopes and fears for that most precious asset — their children. "We don't have a voice," laments Clare Elwood, a London, Ontario, parent, discouraged by the frustrating exercise of seeking answers from the school on her ten-year-old son's progress. "It's like attacking Ma Bell. You don't know where to start, you get shifted from one person to another and you never seem able to grapple with it."

Like Elwood, many Canadians are instinctively suspicious about the potential abuse of power by a monopoly (the power of one) or oligopoly (the power of the few). Too often, such powerful enterprises can ignore the consumer and behave in a complacent and aloof manner. Though government and corporate monopolies and oligopolies have played a big part in Canada's history, the same forces of global economic restructuring are at work close to home. Government privatization of public enterprises such as Air Canada and Petro-Canada, deregulation of financial institutions, competition among long-distance telephone carriers and new players in the beer market are all signs that the economy is undergoing a significant facelift.

The recent decision of federal regulators to lift restrictions on long-distance phone service, like the liberalization of banking rules in the 1980s, which opened the door to foreign competitors, has shaken up a market long dominated by one Canadian giant. Spurred by the arrival of new competitors, Bell Canada has been prodded to offer cheaper long-distance rates to customers who now have the option to choose among several services. In another sector of the economy, the struggle to save financially troubled Canadian Airlines has been motivated not only by a desire to save jobs but by concern about the risks of monopoly power. Canadian's customers legitimately fear reduced service and higher prices if Air Canada emerges as the sole national carrier for the domestic market. To maintain some semblance of domestic competition, there are those who advocate selling a portion of Canadian to a U.S. carrier.

Like these corporate behemoths, large public bureaucracies now face the same uncomfortable process of transformation.[1] Chronic budget deficits, changing demographics, an economic recession and a taxpayer backlash are all putting pressure on governments to rethink the way they deliver services. Now, in addition, there is another factor. Historically, Canadians have looked to government as the fixer of first, not last, resort. But in the 1990s, battered by a lingering economic recession that has wiped out industries, Canadians demonstrate a growing cynicism about government and its ability to solve society's problems.

In education, as in other public services, the public exhibits a "show me" attitude that embodies a sea change in thinking about government. Even though the education sector has made modest moves to thin its ranks, reduce duplication of services and rein in teacher salaries over the past year, public concern about the quality of the service continues to rise. To date, the steps taken by those who manage the education system fall far short of redistributing the power now wielded by the educational establishment.

As a school board trustee in Toronto, John Doherty witnesses the tug and pull of power at close range. "A central body has had a very strong control of education for a long time. Professionals and people within boards of education...have historically had a very, very strong role in determining what happens and how it happens," says the veteran trustee who represents one of the city's significant immigrant communities. "People have been trying to peel off some of that power [from the central bureaucracy]. The centre's response is 'Wait a minute. Don't go too far on this one.' And at the local level people are saying, 'Well, where is the real power? You haven't really given up any real power yet. Until you have given us some real power, then most of what you are saying is probably just rhetoric.'"

The education system can no longer escape the forces of structural change. Under the current arrangement, the provinces set their own education policies and, save for occasional forays to protect their turf from intrusions from Ottawa, have little history of inter-provincial co-operation. However, the mobility of the population and the inexorable pressures on the country to compete globally are developments prodding the provinces to look beyond their borders. As creatures of the provincial government, local school boards carry out broad ministry guidelines as part of their day-to-day management of the system at the local level. The lines of authority between ministries and boards blur when they both have a role in funding, curriculum and other policy issues. Both levels of government, however, are top-down bureaucracies that are not designed to receive and incorporate feedback from the public. Indeed, there are few consequences for politicians and bureaucrats at either level if schools turn in a desultory performance from year to year. Over the past year, for example, angry taxpayers have vented their spleen over trustee salaries, but curriculum policy reforms and school breakfast programs, by contrast, inspired no similar display of public emotion.

An overhaul of the traditional structure of education would create two new poles of influence — at the expense of ministry and school board bureaucracies. With a public consensus on national standards in education, for example, the provinces would be under pressure to adapt policies accordingly. With parents and others given authority to make decisions about their school, school boards would lose one of their most compelling reasons to exist. Indeed, boards as we know them might disappear altogether.

For all the promises of change emanating from school bureaucracies across the country, Canada remains relatively immune to reforms that would break the educational insiders' hold on power. In the United States and Britain, however, the direction is clear: Traditional education bureaucracies are being forced to surrender some of their authority over schools to local communities. In 1992, building on reforms introduced in 1988, the British government issued proposals to give parents more control over the management of local schools and, in the process, kill off local boards.[2] In the United States, similarly radical ideas are bubbling at both federal and state levels. Minnesota, California, New Jersey and other states are on their way to creating so-called "charter schools," which give new players — parents, teachers and community members — the right to set up alternative schools funded by the state but free of the bureaucratic rules faced by other public schools.[3] As in Britain, these new public schools seek to make public education more responsive to client demands. And in the United States, the states and the federal government (which, unlike Canada, has a con-stitutionally recognized role in education) got together in 1990 to generate a shared vision of a new future for education.[4] One of the prominent leaders in that exercise was Bill Clinton, then governor of Arkansas and now U.S. president.

Global Vision

While many parents press for more local control, members of the business community express mounting concern over the lack of expectations and achievements of Canada's schools. Eric Newell, CEO and president of Syncrude Canada, speaks for many when he writes:

> In Canada, we must recognize the forces of global competition and the role of science and technology in reducing costs,

improving reliability and quality. Our economic prosperity and standard of living depend on our ability to compete in the world and to that extent we must be open to the lessons of the international community....There is growing concern [in the business community] for the quality of education, particularly that obtained by those students who do not proceed to post-secondary education.[5]

With increasing regularity in the past few years, these sentiments have been expressed by other members of the business community and their organizations. In 1992, the members of the federal Steering Group on Prosperity focused their attention on the need to create what they describe as a "stronger learning culture in Canada." The emphasis of their report, *Inventing Our Future*, is on the *universal* need for knowledge and skill, on the need for Canadians to be globally competitive and on the need for a *national* forum on learning.[6]

At first glance, the business community's call for national action on education with an international perspective would seem to be at odds with the interests of parents bent on playing a more influential role in decisions about the schooling of their children. Indeed, some might argue that the present structure, with power concentrated in provincial ministries and school boards, offers a satisfactory compromise between business demands for common standards and local demands for parental involvement in school decisions. On reflection, the seemingly incompatible demands of corporate interests and parents reinforce one another.

Both interests can be better served by an education system that centralizes decisions about the goals and decentralizes the choice of means. In a global economy in which the rules are set beyond our borders, Canadians need to build a consensus for national standards in education. Local control of individual schools is of no less importance, with parental and community-based commitments to help all children reach most appropriately for high standards. In other words: national ends — local means.

Though seemingly radical for education, the concept of redistributing power is a significant structural trend evident in other areas of the public and private sectors in Canada and other countries. In the economy, for example, national governments are becoming less able to act independently because of international treaty obligations and the rise of powerful corporations with no fixed national identity. The federal government's job-training strategy is indicative of the twin pressures to centralize and decentralize at the same time. The new Canadian Labour Force Development Board, for example, is supposed to advise the government on policies to promote retraining of workers for the new economy. At the same time, though, new local training boards are expected to adapt the broad policies to the needs of the community.

The corporate world got its own wake-up call some time ago. Powerful economic forces over the past decade, in particular, have forced large bureaucratic companies to rethink the way they do business. The removal of foreign trade barriers and financial restrictions at the international level, coupled with deregulation in many sectors of the economy at home, packs a one-two punch marked "competition." The arrogance of big business with a complacent we-know-best attitude is now unacceptable and unprofitable for companies bent on redefining themselves, whatever the industry, as providers of services. The move to restructure, refocus and reduce, designed to adapt both to global competition and the demands of the local customer, is a painful exercise conducted in the name of corporate survival.

In other sectors, the imperative to think globally and act locally is transforming how individuals think about society. On environmental issues, for example, pollution is a worldwide phenomenon but recycling is now a daily habit for Canadians as their contribution to reducing waste. In the same way, the education sector must rethink its traditional decision-making structures to adjust to new conditions in the world economy and the local community. By redistributing the locus of power, Canadians can identify the education goals and standards needed to adapt to the competitive pressures of the global economy and, equally important, implement programs and practices at the local level to equip every student for the uncertainties ahead.

Even with a shift in decision making, the education system still would retain the most valuable characteristics of a government service: universality. The parallels with health care are compelling. Canadians are justly proud of a publicly financed national health-care system with universal access for all. Like health care, the education system should operate as a public service with access guaranteed for all regardless of their ability to pay.

The integrity of public education is not defined by the presence of a government bureaucracy but by the principles of public funding and open access. These two characteristics can be found in private institutions as well, blurring the distinction between public and private services.[7] The Canadian health-care system is one example in which public funding does not preclude the private delivery of individual services. Many Canadians' doctors are self-employed, with private practices offering services to the general public based on fees negotiated with the government. An individual who does not like the services of one doctor can seek out another physician without financial penalty. The same mix of public and private features can be found in such utilities as Air Canada, Canada Post and universities and colleges in Canada.

Given the challenge for education to centralize its goals and decentralize the means, how can this redistribution of decision making improve the clarity, integrity and accountability of the system? There is no single — or simple — blueprint. Indeed, past reforms have failed in no small measure because they promised single-shot solutions that missed the mark. "So many educational ideas and innovations have been tried over the last two decades, evaluated, and shown to be less than ideal," observes the Paris-based Organization for Economic Co-operation and Development in a 1989 study entitled *Schools and Quality.*[8] "There exists today an 'informed skepticism' about educational change that distinguishes the 1980s from the 1960s and has led to the declining appeal of grand principles and all embracing education theories."

Without imposing a blueprint, however, there are some features common to "made in Canada" reforms that seek to redistribute power: independence (local autonomy), choice and diversity. These are the modifications needed to give those outside the education system a larger political role. In the current wave of education reforms in Canada, provincial ministries and school boards invoke at least the spirit of local autonomy. In practice, the promised decentralization invariably falls short of ceding real political power to those who depend on the provision of sound education services.

Local Autonomy

Across the country, the tide of education reform now runs towards greater local autonomy for schools. Under the rubric of "school-based decision making" (also known as site-based management), some administrative and budget decisions are being shifted to the local school. As a result, the school principal, teachers and parents have more influence on decisions about deploying scarce resources.

The province of Québec has legislated the creation of school advisory councils, comprising elected parents and teachers, who must draft a statement of school philosophy. In addition, parents must be consulted on the criteria for selecting the school principal. "The consultation process has become part of our culture," declares John Killingbeck, acting director general of the Lakeshore School Board on the Island of Montréal. "When goodwill and clear goals exist, positive outcomes occur." In contrast to Québec, recent legislation in Alberta and British Columbia does not require the formation of elected school councils.

The proliferation of these new bodies, though more influential than traditional home and school organizations, creates the impression of a transformation in the structure of the system. In reality, there is less here than meets the eye, since the ministry and/or school board still retains central control over curriculum and funding. Parents, teachers and principals, though more involved in decisions than in the past, are still no more than advisors, at best, in budget and staffing decisions at the local school.

One of the boldest experiments in local autonomy in Canada is taking place in Edmonton, Alberta, where the public board of education has decentralized administrative authority. The school principal now acts more like an entrepreneur than an education bureaucrat. The local school, for example, is not required to use math consultants supplied by the Edmonton board. Instead, the principal can turn to outside suppliers, such as university faculties of education or curriculum experts elsewhere who may have programs more relevant to local needs. Working with a board-allotted budget tied to student enrolment, the principal is able to make spending choices that reflect local priorities established in consultation with parents and teachers.

The promising trend to local autonomy still falls short of the fundamental restructuring of the system taking place in other countries. In New Zealand, for example, faced with a severe budget crisis brought on by changes in the global economy, the government eliminated elementary school boards two years ago. "The gun was to their head, now it's to ours," warns Steve Lawton, a professor of education at the Ontario Institute for Studies in Education, a research and graduate studies centre in Toronto. Like New Zealand, Canada faces having to make uncomfortable choices about a range of public services in an environment of chronic, and rising, budget deficits. Put bluntly, Canadians can no longer afford the current superstructure in education, with layers of decision making that make the system unresponsive both to global change and local demand.

In the current environment of tight budgets, ministries and school boards now have a financial incentive to give more decision-making authority to local schools — leaving them to make the hard choices about possible cuts in programs and services. Toronto trustee Doherty explains, "If you want people to buy into difficult choices, they have got to see what financial shape you're in. They need to have some role to play in the decision making." Like many trustees, he favours the creation of elected school councils so that they make some of the tough choices. "I would like to see them be presented with a [school] budget and have it open for debate."

For Canadian parents, students, taxpayers and employers to have a real say in the running of their schools, provincial ministries would have to decentralize political as well as administrative authority from boards to the local school. As the new political entity, the elected community school council — not the school board — would make decisions about the budget allotted by the province. The local body, of course, would have to abide by certain common principles, such as equal opportunities for all students, and carry out curriculum and other school programs so that students meet educational standards set at the provincial and national levels. To the extent that school boards continue to exist at all — and that need is debatable — they would operate as slimmed-down agencies providing common services — such as transportation, payroll and staff development — to local schools. Provincial ministries, by contrast, would retain their authority to set broad policy directions in education. Where they do not already conduct teacher salary negotiations, the provinces would take on that job from school boards.

A shift in political power from boards to local schools sets the stage for the kind of community-level discussion of educational values and standards now absent in many jurisdictions in Canada. Such a structural transformation will not be easy. It will not happen overnight and, indeed, parents and others in the community will need training and other support to help them take on their new responsibilities. The success of such a redistribution of power rests fundamentally on an active participation by all members of the community — not just middle-class parents or the single-interest groups who now invest considerable time and energy in school affairs. Such personal commitment is the common thread that runs through reforms in Britain and the United States aimed at decentralizing power to the local community. At a time when single parents and, for that matter, two-income families are stretched to meet the daily demands of life, the challenge to become politically involved in local schools should not be taken lightly.

Two American advocates of local autonomy for schools warn against grasping at decentralization by itself as a cure for what ails the system. "Our reform is not school based decision making alone," cautions Robert Sexton, executive director of the Prichard Committee for Academic Excellence, a major public interest advocate for the state of Kentucky's legislated move to local autonomy for schools. In addition to school-based management, Kentucky's 1990 reform created new state agencies to set state-wide goals for education and establish new, progressive programs for evaluating whether the goals have been met. Local councils work well, Sexton cautions, only "where there is strong and informed and sensitive leadership by principals." Fred Hess, executive director of the Chicago Panel on Public School Policy and Finance, another strong proponent of local autonomy, echoes Sexton's cautions. "I'm not sure I'd talk about any as 'the way' to go," he says. Like Sexton, he observes that principals are the key to bringing local autonomy to life.

Some teacher spokespersons in Canada see a dark side to local autonomy. "You can use decentralization as a cover for reducing costs and expenditures," warns Harvey Weiner, deputy secretary general of the Canadian Teachers' Federation. He describes that phenomenon as "distributing poverty." He argues, correctly, that public schools must provide equality of opportunity for all young people, regardless of their parents' economic and social status.

However, the strong attraction in shifting some decisions to the local level is the potential for breaking the political logjam over education. The absence of a meaningful consensus on what schools should — and should not — be expected to do threatens the traditional underpinnings of public education. The ideals of excellence and equity, now embedded in the system, cannot be realized without a more effective structure for decision making than now exists.

An elected school council is the centrepiece for local control. An elected school council representing the diverse interests of teachers, parents and the community would have to make curriculum and program choices within the budget allocated by the provincial ministry. The potential for conflict is high, given distinctions of class, race, language, religion and political ideology that divide every community. But the importance of attending to the needs of students in a complex age must transcend community differences.

As a more democratic local institution, an elected school council has the potential to place teachers and parents in a new co-operative relationship instead of the current confrontations. Problems of how best to educate students should be shared between parents and teachers — just as they must share in the solutions. While parents still must work out individual differences with teachers, the school council should provide a forum that sets a new tone of shared responsibility.

Choice and Diversity

In an institutional sense, Canadians have a lot of freedom to choose where to educate their children. The kind of public funding available for Catholic and francophone education, for example, has no parallel in the United States, where the strongest advocates of school choice can be found. In Canada, almost all provinces fund Roman Catholic schools and, in several provinces, other minority denominations receive some degree of public support. Prodded by Supreme Court rulings in the late 1980s, the provinces have moved grudgingly to recognize the rights of francophone minorities outside Québec to establish their own publicly funded school boards. Québec already provides funding for its anglophone minority. Over the past twenty-five years, with a blend of federal and provincial funding, French immersion programs have become a major factor in public schools across the country. Indeed, they are in strong demand from middle-class parents anxious to give their children an extra academic edge. One of the unintended consequences of French immersion programs has been the emergence of an informal upper tier in education, largely separating students by income groups. Blue-collar parents have exhibited much less interest in French immersion for their children.

Choice in education takes other forms, too. In many jurisdictions, parents can send their children outside their own community so long as the school in question has met the demand of parents in its geographical area; for example, within Metro Toronto, students in the city of York attend schools in Toronto that may offer a particular program not offered by their own school. Alternative schools, dating back to the 1960s when left-wing parents demanded more control over their schools, still put a high premium on parental involvement. But they also have matured into more mainstream institutions that reflect the more conservative political climate of the 1990s. Still another vehicle for choice is the magnet school, which offers special services in selected subject areas, such as the arts and sciences.

Yet many parents are still dissatisfied with the level of choice. In some cases, attendance at publicly funded Roman Catholic schools — which differ from other public schools in their perceived commitment to discipline and their freedom to teach moral and religious values — is restricted to students of that faith. Even when non-Catholics can send their children to such schools, they and Catholic parents complain that their schools are underfunded relative to other public schools. However, the major complaint of parents is that public schools generally teach the same curriculum, practise similar teaching techniques and live by the same education philosophy. Recent Supreme Court rulings that prohibit teaching about one religious denomination to the exclusion of others (a privilege still granted Roman Catholic schools) incense some parents who feel that public education is shirking its responsibility to teach morals and values.

Given these and other concerns, the challenge for public education is to create a wider menu of choices for parents. Just as schools must be liberated from the bureaucratic control of school boards, parents must have more freedom to choose where to educate their children. The education system must respond to the issue of choice or risk losing public support.

The choice issue ignites deep passions. In the United States, where the debate has an especially ideological tinge, supporters paint a simplistic picture of a market-driven system that will force under-performing schools to shape up or close down. Detractors, many of them teachers and school administrators, create a similarly misleading impression that public education will collapse under the weight of choice. The truth lies somewhere in between these extremes. Pro-choice advocate Chester Finn argues that "parents are more engaged, the educators in the school are more apt to collaborate with each other, the match between teacher strengths and pupil needs is improved, and the school itself becomes a self-renewing system that gets ample feedback from its clientele and has the capacity to adjust and improve what it is doing."[9]

The spectre of all-out competition among schools raises justifiable concerns. Education is too vital a public service to be treated as if it were a commodity like hamburger. Choice should not be used as a stick to beat schools into promoting themselves as "McSchool vs. Learner King," as if they were purveyors of budget-priced products served with uniform slickness by minimum-wage personnel. A more relevant comparison, however, already exists in post-secondary education in Canada. Community colleges and universities compete for students based on a variety of non-price factors, such as size, academic programs, the quality of undergraduate life and graduate studies. Where possible, elementary and secondary schools should be encouraged to demonstrate their strengths, with freedom to specialize on the basis of academic and other programs. At present, schools have little incentive to differentiate themselves in ways that communicate educational values to the public.

The reality of an increasingly multicultural society means that the education system must address the issue of school choice. Parents today are less willing to accept a "one-size-fits-all" approach to education that fails to acknowledge differences in cultural values, academic orientation, teaching practices and learning styles. Past the shouting of predictable antagonists in the argument today are legitimate but complex questions about how choice contributes to raising educational quality and standards — for all students.

The essential point is to help parents make more informed choices about schools, based on a variety of criteria, including programs and teaching practices best suited to their children. On its own, freedom of choice will not reform the school system.[10] Parents, for example, are not always wise consumers. Some lack the time or interest to make well-considered choices; others, regrettably, are absent from the scene altogether. Moreover, the formula for student success is not a simple one, the result of a combination of factors that relate to the school, home and students themselves. A school that sets high expectations, for example, delivers a compelling message about its commitment to students.

These caveats are not grounds to dismiss the case for school choice. Rather, they suggest why schools must communicate more effectively with parents and others about the conditions necessary for an effective learning environment. Ultimately, the public needs to know much more about why some schools do well so that others can learn from success. Other things being equal, parents and students will prefer to stick with their neighbourhood schools; the schools need to give them a reason to do so.

For school choice to be meaningful, there must be greater differentiation among schools. Some might focus on traditional teaching strategies, while others offer the latest experiments in integrated curriculum. Some might stress languages, others fine arts and still others math and sciences.

To be sure, all schools would have to fulfil certain require-ments to meet broad education policies and goals established by the province. But public schools have much to learn from the best prac-tices of alternative schools, which offer a well-defined philosophy, a strong commitment to parental involvement and specialty courses to enrich the academic and vocational experiences of students. On a positive note, some public schools — in conjunction with parents and teachers — are drafting statements of goals and expectations. This a good beginning. The second step is to give players at the local level some political clout through the establishment of school coun-cils. In this way, parents and others at the local level will be able to work co-operatively to ensure that good intentions translate into stronger student performance over time. Steady improvement in student success is the best testimonial for raising public confidence in the future of Canadian schools.

But, like school choice, increased diversity for schools raises some difficult questions. In short, how much diversity is too much? Public schools are the one institution expected to serve all members of society and communicate a sense of what it means to be Canadian. In the wake of the 1992 Yonge Street disturbances, a fed-eral task force recommended the creation of several black-only schools to combat high drop-out levels among black youths. The proposal smacks of segregation, separating black youth already alienated by mainstream society. Diversity cannot be used as a back-door route to discriminate against those who already are dis-enfranchised. Instead, the principle of diversity should be honoured in other ways — through special programs targeted at minorities and the poor, who face too many hurdles on their way through school. Alternative and "magnet" schools are good examples of "niche" marketing, with a clear focus on goals and values. But much more needs to be done — in Ontario, for example, only 80 out of

4,000 public schools are alternatives, a drop in the bucket given the public demand for a wider range of educational options.

Any effort to increase diversity among local schools must also come to grips with the thorny political issue of public funding for private schools. Ontario has long rejected public funding for denominational schools, for example, with the notable exception of Catholic education. A 1985 report to the government by Bernard Shapiro, then director of the Ontario Institute for Studies in Education, urged the extension of public funding to other private and religious schools provided they met certain conditions, including accessibility.[11] His recommendations were shelved by the government of the day for financial reasons and because the issue is politically divisive.

In British Columbia and Alberta, by contrast, religious and other alternative schools receive some public funding provided they, too, meet certain provincial criteria. In Newfoundland, for historical reasons, schools operated by four religious denominations (Anglican, Roman Catholic, Pentecostal and Salvation Army) as well as the so-called public (secular) schools receive funding from tax revenues. There is no moral justification in a multicultural, multireligious country such as Canada to deny some parents the right to send their children to schools whose values and traditions conform to their own. The choices are quite simple: either no public funding for any denominational school or equal treatment in the school system for all religious groups.

In a reinvented education system, the line would blur between public and private schools. Under a system that encourages diversity, all schools would be eligible for public funds, subject to certain basic criteria. All such schools would have to abide by common principles of equal access, respect for gender and minority rights, and minimum education standards. Without such principles, the danger is that diversity produces an unpalatable system of "separate but equal" schools. In other words, publicly funded denominational or other "private" schools could not deny access to any child who wished to attend. The choice system cannot be used to sort or even segregate students on religious, racial or cultural grounds. Moreover, diversity must offer real choice among excellent schools representing a range of well-defined missions. Just as with health care in Canada, "public" education could evolve into a network of "independent" institutions supported through a system of public funding.

Conclusion

We have proposed here a radical simplification of the present bureaucratic system, one that is designed to give parents and members of the community more say in the life of their school. The role of provincial ministries of education would be cut back to that of setting policy and providing financial resources. Such a reorganization, eliminating as it does the need for elected school boards, would also clarify where responsibility lies for all educational decisions.

The test of a system's accountability is its openness. As things are, clarity about who is really in charge is one of the missing elements in education. A reinvented system that places the responsibility for standards and resources clearly at the national and provincial levels and puts all aspects of school operations, including curriculum, staffing, and student learning at the school level, is clear about its responsibilities. Moreover, when decisions about schools are made by local councils, sensitive to local needs, the system becomes open and accountable, too.

Changing the way schools are run will take courage and patience. But such is the challenge for all Canadians who care about creating more responsive, effective schools for the future. Parents and others who want to take back their schools must contribute their time and effort to negotiating a consensus on goals and expectations at the level of the school, the province and the nation. In the process, parents, business and other members of the public will have to become better informed consumers of education. The sacrifice is high, but so, too, are the rewards.

Chapter 4

Redefining School

*I*n *the frontier* town of Vanderhoof in central British Columbia, traditional ideas about school are getting a face-lift. "Black Bob's University," so named for its location in a former arcade, is an adult learning centre for high school drop-outs and adult students operated by the Nechako School District. As an alternative setting for those uncomfortable about returning to a regular classroom, the centre enables students to study for their high school certificate at their own pace, under step-by-step instructions of computer-assisted learning programs. The teacher serves in a supporting role to assist students, who must master the material in one phase before moving to the next.

Carol Krawcyk, a mother of two children in high school, jumped at the opportunity to return to school on her own terms. "It's too bad it took me that many years to mature," says Krawcyk, who pays no tuition fees to study Grade 12 math, biology and history. She also likes setting a positive example for her children. "It's important as a parent to encourage your kids," she says during a break from the computer. "I never had that encouragement."

With funding assistance from the B.C. and federal governments, the Nechako board also worked with native leaders to locate the same computer-assisted education program on a reserve in nearby Fort St. John. Since native students account for a disproportionate share of high school drop-outs in the area, school officials and native leaders created a classroom beside the band council office on the reserve. Maddy Moberly says the unconventional setting enables her to finish her education in a non-threatening environment. "You don't feel embarrassed that you're twenty years old and still in Grade 11," she says. "It would be a little uncomfortable in a regular school." In another experiment, several native schools in the district operate four days a week with longer hours, a scheduling strategy designed to reduce the previously high rates of absenteeism.

Meanwhile, at the high school in Vanderhoof, students participate in activities not offered twenty years ago when Carol Krawcyk was a teenager. During the school year, as part of a partnership between the school board and local business, students visit dairy farms and forestry and other resource companies to get hands-on experience and learn about possible careers. For seventeen-year-old Morgan Minty, the school's one-week-long "Project Heavy Duty," a partnership with local business, gave him first-hand experience in the local forestry industry. During the week, Minty says he made new connections between life at school and on the job. "You can't keep the two separate," he concludes. "Without high school you can't get a job." The Grade 12 student also made a personal discovery during Project Heavy Duty. After one day driving gravel and log trucks, Minty decided he had no wish to become a truck driver!

In Vanderhoof, as in other communities, the definition of school is beginning to change. In Edmonton, Toronto and other urban centres, some schools now offer classes in shopping malls to reach drop-outs on their own turf. In other communities, the school day is being reorganized to prevent students, especially those making the transition from elementary to secondary school, from getting lost in the cracks. Students spend more time with fewer teachers, for example, to improve discipline, study habits and classroom rapport. To their credit, some Canadian schools are implementing radical new methods to see what works — and what might work — to boost student performance. But these schools are still the exception to the rule of traditional thinking about schools and how they should operate. Nechako school superintendent Mike Fitzpatrick, a one-time school drop-out who brings a missionary's zeal to his work, believes the time has come for schools to break down the walls. "We're in a real paradigm shift in many areas," he says. "The industrial model of school is falling apart."

Fitzpatrick is not the first to describe schools as operating with an "industrial" or "factory" model. The label is becoming more and more common as educators and others have come to realize that educational institutions designed in the latter part of the nineteenth century embody the ideals, beliefs and values of that period. The notable success of the time had been the invention of mass production in which a vast army of relatively unskilled workers, operating to a minutely detailed plan, worked with standard components to assemble a final product of standard specifications. The whole enterprise was overseen by a handful of managers and foremen who were accountable to the factory owners for the overall output.

The apparent success of this system of industrial production seemed to provide a natural model for systems of mass public education, then being created in many countries for the first time.

School boards (owners), superintendents and principals (managers and foremen) supervised relatively uneducated workers (teachers) in the task of producing basically educated children in batch lots of thirty or so at a time. The "spoilage" or drop-out rate was always fairly high but with the variable quality of raw material, this was seen as acceptable. Although schools have improved significantly in their productivity over the past century, the basic model — a rigid, rule-bound bureaucracy — has changed little since the advent of mass education a century ago.

Today, the assumptions of the old model have been rejected by many industrial enterprises and now they are being questioned in education also; for example, the school year is still based on the needs of an agrarian society that relied on young people to help with the summer harvest. The school day assumes a family structure in which one parent, namely the mother, is home to greet the children when they return from school. Even today's classrooms look much like those of 100 years ago: the blackboard and chalk, the desks for the most part in rows, and a teacher standing at the front of the room dispensing most of the information. As American author George Leonard observed in *The Atlantic Monthly* recently, "We can no longer improve the education of our children by improving school as we know it. The time has come to recognize that school is not the solution. It is the problem."[1]

In Canada, the educational establishment is only beginning to take tentative steps to rethink its basic ideas and assumptions about school. The demands of an increasingly multicultural student population, the political imperative to put a lid on education spending and the shifting demands of the workplace are only some of the pressures on schools to look at themselves in a new light. Such a re-evaluation requires a complete turn-about in thinking about the rationale for school, one that shifts the emphasis from what teachers do to what students do, from teaching to learning, and from a focus on educational "inputs" to one on "outcomes" — what students learn.

This new way of looking at the educational enterprise sets the stage for students to shoulder more responsibility for their own education. This, in turn, will give teachers more opportunities to find strategies for achieving better results in the classroom and to provide individual support for students who need it. The focus of the school and the basis for its accountability will be its results rather than the effort it makes.

Learning: The Essence of Schooling

For most students, education is carried on in a highly regimented, artificial environment. Yet, out of this rigid setting, students are expected to blossom into self-motivated, creative individuals imbued with a love of learning throughout their lives. What is more, the current design of most school days assumes that students will acquire knowledge and skills in ways that bear no relationship to the way they normally learn. The student experience is regimented in forty-five-to-fifty-minute chunks of time, with breaks punctuated by the bell. High school students move from class to class, from teacher to teacher, each of whom is responsible for a discrete segment of the curriculum. Teachers have little time to co-ordinate with each other, collaborate on lessons or confer about student performance and effective teaching strategies. U.S. educational reformer Ted Sizer rightfully asks, "Who does their most creative intellectual work in forty-five-minute snippets?"[2] The organization of the school day may suit the administrative requirements of school officials but may not satisfy the diverse learning styles of an increasingly heterogeneous student population. The semester system takes the disjointed curriculum to even greater extremes. A student may take a language course for four months and then drop it, only to try to pick it up again eight months later.

Some students may learn in spite of the system, but what of the others? The current structure of school subverts the very idea of learning when the supposed objective is to develop students with new kinds of skills. Sitting passively while the teacher imparts abstract ideas is a model for one type of learning experience, but it is not the only route to knowledge. In the real world, one is not penalized for making mistakes while one is still in training; rather, the challenge is to figure out what went wrong and look for the right answer. If one person takes longer than another to find a solution, so be it.

A different rationale applies in school, namely that all students are given the same period of time to cover a given amount of material. Those who are successful are given high marks and those who are less so are given fewer. Once this pattern is repeated often enough, those whose learning style or rate leads them to receive consistently lower marks get the message that school is not the place where they will succeed. The first step on the road to dropping out has been taken.

U.S. education scholar Lauren Resnick of the University of Pittsburgh has studied some of the inconsistencies of the education system. She observes that school learning tends to be intellectual, symbolic and generalized, without much opportunity for either teacher or student to make connections between "big ideas" and everyday life. Out-of-school learning, by contrast, usually occurs in a social context, is relative to a specific problem and involves more than one person looking for the solution.[3] One builds a garage, for example, according to building codes approved by the municipality, relying on friends and neighbours to complete the project.

Like the garage builder, schools are beginning to recognize the merits of learning based on team work, hands-on activities, relevance to the "real world" and the ability to think analytically. The employability skills profile published by the Conference Board of Canada puts a premium on graduates able to think independently and work co-operatively.[4] Other business groups are sending the same message that they want a new kind of graduate. But traditional methods of schooling — rote learning, the teacher as master — are not adequate to enable students to acquire the new competencies demanded by business.

In line with this way of thinking, a royal commission on education in British Columbia recommended a new approach to teaching and learning. The controversial reforms put students at centre stage and propose reorganizing the curriculum in ways that emphasize process over content.[5] As a result, according to the reformers, students will learn how to gather, synthesize and analyze information instead of being told what to think by the teacher. Provincial education officials argue that, given the demands of an information-service economy of the twenty-first century, schools must create learning environments that encourage students to think for themselves. The teacher is a guide, students learn in groups, and subject disciplines give way to new courses that link ideas across the curriculum. The B.C. reforms have drawn both praise and criticism, with business and parents uncertain whether the new ways will achieve stronger results.

Keith Gray, a vice-president of the Business Council of British Columbia, voices the ambivalence felt in many quarters. "There is a lot of very good teaching going on," he says, applauding some aspects of the province's reforms. "The changes seem to be more learner-focused. That shift in emphasis is fine from a business point of view," he cautions, "so long as the individual is learning and is being evaluated through the process and is obtaining those skills."

Gray's concern underscores a central conflict in education: Who's in charge? Putting the learner first is liberating for students, but will that freedom be abused? There is no single design for reinvented schools. Indeed, there should be many designs that demonstrate "what works" in a variety of circumstances. But schools that put a new focus on the learner have some features in common. These include effective use of time, viewing the community as a resource for learning, and planning a broad menu of teaching strategies and technologies to support learning. Let's look more closely at these characteristics.

Time and Learning

Canada's mediocre showing in recent international comparisons of educational achievement has sparked interest in how much time students should spend in school. Would a longer school day improve results? Would a longer school year guarantee increased academic achievement? The short answer to both questions is no. Just as spending more money on education does not guarantee better results, neither will spending more time in school. How *well* the money and the time are spent is the real criterion.

The results of the 1992 International Assessment of Educational Progress illustrate the point. A comparison of the performance of thirteen-year-olds in math and science in twenty countries reveals no apparent systematic relationship between instructional time and success in science (see Table 1).[6] U.S. students who logged an average of 1,002 hours of class time in science stood at the back of the pack, while Korean students with 977 hours of science instruction topped the list. With an average twenty-two fewer hours of instruction than the Koreans, Canadian students ranked in the middle. Critics of Canadian education lament that students here spend less time in school relative to other countries, but that comparison provides insufficient information to draw helpful conclusions.

Table 1: Instructional Time in Selected Countries

Country in order of student achievement in science	Average number of instructional days per year	Average number of instructional minutes per day	Average number of hours of instruction per year
Korea	222	264	977
Taiwan	222	318	1177
Hungary	177	223	658
Canada	188	304	953
France	174	370	1073
England	192	300	960
China	251	305	1276
United States	178	338	1002

Harold Stevenson, an educational researcher at the University of Michigan who has studied educational practices in Asian and American schools over the past decade, shows how the often-quoted comparison of time in school can be misleading;[7] for example, in Asian schools, although children spend more hours in the school building each day, their lunch breaks, recesses and other time spent out of the classroom are all longer than in the typical American school. Also, the supposedly greater number of school days includes Saturdays, when often only a half day is spent in school. The Economic Council of Canada, in its 1992 study on education and training in Canada entitled *A Lot to Learn*, concludes that "the longer school year would not, by itself, lead to higher achievement, unless it were accompanied by a better use of the school day."[8]

In New Brunswick, an independent commission on education reform urged the government to lengthen the school year as part of a large package of measures to raise standards and performance. The government deftly sidestepped a direct confrontation with the teachers' union, which adamantly opposed extension of the school year. Instead, the government reassigned five days within the contract so that more time is devoted to instructional purposes. Teachers retain their professional development days, but school boards have less flexibility to close schools for bad weather or school trips. As a result, schools have more time for core subjects, especially math and English, as required by the province's curriculum reforms.

The issue of time is a political sore point in education. With just cause, the public suspects that schools, in broadening their mandate over the past twenty years, have given short shrift to the fundamentals of literacy and numeracy. If consumers are to regain confidence in public education, school officials must provide tangible evidence to show that schools can deliver solid, measurable results. Consequently, *how* students spend their time, on what activities, becomes a touchstone for judging quality. Conservative reformers who demand a return to the basics want schools to narrow their focus, with more time devoted to the fundamentals of literacy and math. By contrast, school officials who espouse the "new basics" required for the flexible, creative thinker see the need for time to be used in more innovative ways. The way out of this dilemma is to think about the relationship between time and learning quite differently.

Traditionally, the quantity of a student's schooling has been measured in "contact hours" — literally, hours in contact with a teacher. Time is fixed; learning is the variable. All students spend the same period of time in a course, but they do not all acquire the same amount of knowledge. Such an outcome is consistent with the factory model of education, in which some students prosper and others fall by the wayside. To give meaning to the goal of educational excellence for all students, the traditional relationship between time and academic achievement needs to be reversed. In short, we should make *learning the constant, and time the variable*. In that way, schools would recognize in practice what is already accepted in principle: that individuals learn at different rates. Instead of succumbing to the artificial strictures of time, teachers would have more room to experiment with alternative strategies to help students learn more effectively. What should be of prime importance is that students reach their educational destination, regardless of the fact that some arrive sooner than others.

In the shift in thinking that puts the learner first, schools must accept a crucial corollary: *Students must master the required skills and knowledge.* The current school structure is designed on the assumption that all students take the same amount of time for a subject, with the focus on getting through the material. What naturally alarms parents and others are innovations in the use of time that give flexibility without much semblance of form; for example, many schools now promote students in the early years of elementary school regardless of their academic performance. The policy is based on research that shows that students held back to repeat a grade run a high risk of dropping out later. But students are not well served if, in the name of "age-appropriate" grouping, they are simply promoted without adequate skills and knowledge to progress at the next level. Privately, school officials concede they must do a better job in remedial and related support to ensure that students have the tools they need to survive and prosper in school.

British Columbia's attempts to phase out traditional grades, as part of its education reform package, aims at putting a new emphasis on learning. In elementary school, the province has moved to multi-grade classrooms to create more flexibility for individual students. Thus students who are strong in one subject can move on to more challenging material, which would not otherwise have been available until the next grade. At the same time, they may be weak in another subject, requiring extra help to grasp the material. Although parents recognize that the same student can be strong in one subject and weak in another, they are uneasy about groupings that, they suspect, will demand less of students in the end.

Other countries are already experimenting with teaching and learning techniques that rearrange the allotted hours of the school day to benefit the learner. The Köln-Holweide Comprehensive School in Cologne, Germany, has been successful in adjusting the pace at which students move through school.[9] A team of teachers works with the same 120 students throughout their school career. The teaching team makes decisions about the best use of instructional time, making adjustments to suit the needs of individual students, who vary in age and ability. Students work in small groups of six to eight and progress at their own pace. Teachers work co-operatively to support each other's efforts in the classroom. The result is a drop-out rate of 1 per cent compared to a national average of 14 per cent.

A natural corollary to changes in the school day is to modify the length of the school year. The original demands of the agrarian economy for which the school year was designed have long since disappeared. In some parts of the United States and Canada, experiments are under way to implement year-round schooling. The U.S. National Association for Year-Round Education estimates that, in the United States, 736,000 students in more than 870 schools attended class twelve months a year in 1990-91.[10]

In Canada, the trend is less dramatic. North York, Ontario, for example, has three year-round schools that allow greater flexibility for adult learners. Other schools offering heritage language and community programs are open seven days a week. In British Columbia, school boards facing a rapidly expanding population are looking at year-round schooling as a way to ease crowding. The Central Okanagan District has requested implementation funding from the provincial ministry for year-round schools and in Williams Lake, in the Cariboo-Chilcotin District, one elementary school offers a year-round program to attract students from nearby overcrowded schools. The attraction of year-round schooling is smaller classes (with reduced teacher burn-out in consequence), less absenteeism and more flexibility for parents with seasonal jobs to spend more time with their children. On the downside, year-round schooling is complex to administer, adds costs for air conditioning and transportation and requires changes in contracts with staff accustomed to a ten-month year.

Much of the drive for year-round operations is economic, with a view to more effective use of buildings and equipment. The proliferation in demands on schools — and they are not likely to diminish — gives added appeal to the idea of school twelve months a year. Remediation, summer school, supplementary language programs, enrichment programs, are all essential for students who want to make up for lost time or to press ahead with their studies. With a growing number of students dropping back into school, traditional notions of when and how schooling occurs — and for whom — no longer apply. Instead, the structure of the school day and year should be shaped by the needs of the learner, not by administrative efficiency or professional convenience.

Learning from the Community

The style in which a school is built often conveys its own message about its place in the community and in the lives of the students that attend. Older, inner-city schools built at the end of the nineteenth century often have windows that are large enough to admit light but high enough to ensure that children cannot see out. This style reached its extreme form in the mid-1960s, when schools with no windows at all became quite common.

With or without windows, schools have traditionally been places where the focus of children's attention was kept strictly inside. In recognition of their custodial function, schools have always placed primary attention on keeping their students within the confines of the school, except for carefully planned and guided excursions. Obviously, schools do have a guardian role, especially with young children, but this concern to keep track of students physically seems also to have an intellectual counterpart, the value of which is much more debatable.

Computers are beginning to break down the walls of schools and allow learners to gain access to the world of knowledge. Too often, however, those same walls place strict limits on the scope of student learning. Schools may be in the physical sense a part of their community, but intellectually they are too often apart from it — removed in a cloud of abstraction that makes them irrelevant to many learners and frustratingly distant from other members of the community. This intellectual "distance" can work both ways. Schools need to interact more with their communities in ways that will increase the relevance of what they do and in ways that will draw on community resources to support learning. However, there are also some communities whose values are such that greater interaction can lead to the stifling of learning opportunities through the banning of books or, worse, the promotion of intolerance towards others.

Nonetheless, there is so much in every community that can support learning on the part of students, from libraries to colleges, from cultural organizations to senior citizens' centres, from businesses to labour unions. The largest-scale application of this principle involves co-op education and work experience being blended with academic study. In Alberta, work is progressing towards apprenticeship schemes involving high school students. There are many students whose readiness to work exceeds their readiness to study, and in these cases, they should not have to choose between work and school. Schemes that allow young people in the sixteen-to-nineteen-year-old range to combine work and study in Canada fall far behind those of Europe. This lack contributes to the unacceptable drop-out rates.

Work and school can be combined in many ways. In a recent review of European innovations in this area conducted for the Brookings Institution, William Nothdurft concludes that "work experience and work-relevant education are the keys to smooth school-to-work transitions."[11] The high schools of the past have been oriented towards students going on to post-secondary education (not coincidentally, the life experience of nearly all of their teachers). The role of the schools in preparing students for the world of work has tended to be somewhat less well defined than their role in preparing students for post-secondary education. As Nothdurft points out, in Sweden, aspects of work experience begin for all students in elementary school and by late high school, some students are spending as much as 60 per cent of their time in the workplace. A work experience component is part of the compulsory curriculum of all high school students in Germany, a country whose apprenticeship system is amongst the best in the world.

But there is more to linking schools to communities than preparation for work. The essence of "environmental" education, of "global" education, of "multicultural" education, of studying "history," "science," or "English," can be the means of coming to understand one's community in all its dimensions. There is too often a sense in which the school experience, while trying to prepare its students for a broad variety of experiences in life, merely abstracts them from the concrete realities in which they live and presents them with something disconnected, irrelevant (to them) and alienating. If school is to be a place worth staying in (for a student), it must be a place where connections are made, where learning is meaningful and where people learn more about coping with the complex realities of their many communities.

Two practical implications of adopting such a view of the school's place in the community emerge, one personal and one technical. On a personal level, if schools are connected closely to the various communities they serve, then members of those communities should have much to contribute to the school curriculum and should be constantly seen as a part of the school. One is reminded of the African proverb "It takes a whole village to educate a child." Second, new information technology has an important role in connecting the learner with the farther reaches of his or her community and with other communities that are not readily accessible. As things are, it is rare even to find a telephone in a school classroom. Yet this is the technology we all use most for making connections and for learning new information all the time.

Teaching Strategies

Education is prone to fads, both creating overblown claims and inviting inevitable scepticism about any new teaching method. The current furor over the best way to teach children to read and write — whether by traditional phonetic spelling ("phonics") or by progressive "whole-language" methods — typifies the emotionalism that fuels a contentious debate over educational achievement.

Yet, for all the controversy, ideas about teaching have changed little over the past century. The most significant exception is the adoption over the past thirty years of a teaching philosophy known as "child-centred learning." While teachers and others endorse an approach that gives students more freedom, sceptics in the back-to-basics movement argue for a more structured approach that puts teachers in control of instruction.

Examples of "child-centred learning" are most visible in the early grades, when children work in groups at "activity centres" instead of sitting in rows of desks. The high school classroom, by contrast, is usually still dominated by teacher-led instruction, worksheets and textbooks. But if the enterprise of schooling is to put learning first, then traditional thinking about what happens in the classroom must be re-examined. Students learn not only at different rates, but in different ways. Accordingly, schools must provide a variety of teaching methods as well as flexible time frames to help students reach agreed outcomes.

Pragmatism — "what works" — rather than ideological commitment — "what the establishment believes in" — should be the basis for adopting teaching strategies. There has been altogether too much debate in education about the "right way" to teach each part of the curriculum. In reality, different methods work in different ways with different students in different circumstances, and few absolute generalizations can be made. For example, math teacher Charles Ledger at Zion Heights Junior High School in North York has won both praise and criticism for his use of "direct instruction" (teacher-led) methods in the classroom. Since the students do well, back-to-basics enthusiasts cite his methods to support their demands for more structured teaching methods. Others are more sceptical, noting that the school itself, in an affluent sector of North York, is academically strong to begin with, and many of the students in the math class have been specially selected.

A more diverse set of schools could offer a clearer menu of alternatives to parents free to choose the school that best conforms to their values and their children's needs. The trouble is that, at present, most schools are not clear about their learning expectations or the measures of results. As a result, alternative methods of teaching become matters of ideology or personal preference instead of being the objects of empirical inquiry.

Reinvented schools should be given every incentive to experiment with both traditional and unconventional ideas in the name of improving results for all students. Some schools in Ontario and British Columbia, for example, are recycling ideas from the 1960s and adapting them to the 1990s. The recently renewed interest in team teaching, especially for students in their early teens, is one example. Given that students in senior elementary and junior high school are the most likely to drop out of school, some schools are now experimenting with team teaching and with groups of students sticking with the same teachers for several years. In this way, it is hoped, fewer students will lose interest in learning.

The furor over streaming, a practice that groups students by perceived levels of ability, can be better understood once effective learning, rather than time and teachers' preferences, becomes the determinant for teaching strategies. The factory model of schooling provided for all students to receive essentially the same teaching for the same amount of time and accepted the inevitable variation in output. A modification of this approach saw lower-achieving students being separated from the main academic stream, supposedly to enhance their chance of success. In reality, the separate stream merely lowered the expectations for learning. Caught in a downward spiral, these students moved to their inevitable academic dead end.

These practices have been shown to have a particularly negative impact on certain groups of students, including racial minorities, students whose mother tongue is not English, children of poor families and students having various disabilities, all of whom are disproportionally represented among high school drop-out statistics. As a result, moves are in progress to destream the high schools, moves that are creating dismay and confusion among people both inside and outside the education field.

The problem to which streaming was thought to be an answer, namely the different rates at which different children learn, requires a fundamentally different response: to make learning the constant and time the variable. Grouping students together without making provisions for individual differences may erase the socially divisive and inequitable practices of the present system. But the practice will be counterproductive without adequate support in the classroom to ensure all students achieve their best. Otherwise, the change may come at the cost of a more general lowering of standards and expectations — the very opposite of what is needed at this time.

Another approach, developed by Henry Levin of Stanford University, is Accelerated Learning.[12] He argues that slow learners, just like so-called gifted students, need an enriched educational environment. His approach, which sets high expectations and offers multi-sensory stimulation for those with learning problems, has had striking success in several schools in California and other U.S. states.

Technology to Support Learning

Technological advances have made possible a much wider variety of learning systems than was the case even twenty years ago, and the full scope of these advances has barely been dreamed about by even the most computer-literate educators. As author Edward Fiske points out, "When new technologies do find their way into the classroom, they tend to be co-opted by the system. Television, to the extent that it is used at all, is plugged-in teacher talk."[13] Computers too, at first, have been used as extensions of the same methods used by teachers. He also cites John Naisbitt who, in *Megatrends*, outlines three stages of technological innovation.[14] Stage one involves applications having no threat to existing patterns of behaviour — in the case of computers in schools, this took the form of electronic games. Stage two, which still dominates, sees the new technology extend or speed up existing methods — computer-assisted instruction. Stage three represents a major change and one that has scarcely been broached in education: when a new technology suggests new activities, new goals and new methods that had not been hitherto contemplated.

Computers are poised to enter that third stage in education, and a few examples have already been seen. National Geographic's work with TERC (the Technical Education Research Center in Cambridge, Massachusetts) to develop the Kid's Network has pioneered children's collaborative research and learning across school and state boundaries. In Canada, Writers in Electronic Residence — the brainchild of Trevor Owen, a Toronto English teacher — is using computer conferencing to allow students to discuss their writing with professional writers. IBM has donated computer labs to several universities to support innovation in the learning of math and science. This program is enabling students at Etobicoke Collegiate to undertake joint science projects with members of York University's Faculty of Science.

But such "third-generation" applications of computers in education require fundamental research and development on a large scale before they can become commonplace. Such large-scale R&D is the vision of Gordon Boddez who, with the support of Alberta Education, has created the Alberta Education Technology Research Foundation, with a mission to explore and develop the potential for information technologies to revolutionize school learning. Boddez dreams of children in school being able to tap into all the programs of the CBC, the films of the NFB, the statistics of Statistics Canada on a digitalized basis from computers located in every classroom. Boddez concludes, "The technology is all there now. All we need is the political will to put it in place, and a vision of truly individualized learning can become a reality."

To be intellectually liberated, one requires access to information beyond that of the school. As George Leonard pointed out in his provocative *Atlantic Monthly* article, "The End of School":

> When computers were first proposed as learning tools, some people were concerned that children would become little robots, plugged in to their machines, isolated from human contact. In most cases just the opposite has happened. Actually the conventional classroom, not the computer, is the isolation cell, the lockup. Contemporary technology, used not as an adjunct to the classroom but as something entirely new, inspires co-operation, encourages learning teams, and builds student confidence.[15]

The networking of computers, now commonplace in offices, is likely to transform schools as we know them within the next two decades.

Teachers, once nervous that computers were a threat to their own professional roles, will see that with the third wave of innovation now under way, computers are supporting learning in ways they had never dreamed of and that are quite beyond their own capacities. Not only are computers the key to students' achievement of their academic goals, they also represent the tool that is transforming every workplace in Canada today. As future workers, therefore, students need to be proficient at using computers much as, in days gone by, they had to be able to write with a pen.

Technology will never be the complete answer to the problems of teaching and learning. Yet compared with other areas of contemporary life, schools have a long way to go in making what is normal elsewhere become commonplace. Students are already more familiar with new technology than their teachers and find a computer to be a natural adjunct to learning. The reinvented school will be more child centred than any of its predecessors because technology holds the key to each student's ability to learn at his or her own pace. And learning is the reason for the school to exist at all.

Chapter 5

Clarifying
the Vision

When Dale and Geraldine Botting moved to Newmarket, Ontario, from Regina, Saskatchewan, in 1986, they posed a seemingly innocent question to teachers at their children's new schools: "What can we expect as the result of their school experiences?" The Bottings were especially concerned about the answer for their youngest child, about to enter Grade 1, because his school featured the latest trends in education: ungraded classrooms and "whole-language" reading methods.

Accustomed to more traditional teaching practices at the schools their two older children had attended in Saskatchewan, the Bottings were stunned by the response of the Ontario schools to their question. "We might have been asking a question in Italian or Greek," says Dale Botting. Teachers and principals were reluctant to discuss curriculum, teaching methods and learning outcomes. "We wanted to know what could we expect at key points in the education process." Instead of candour, the Bottings were met with denials, defensiveness and hostility from school officials. A parent volunteer in her son's Grade 1 classroom, Geraldine Botting was called a "spy" by the teacher when she asked probing questions about teaching methods. When they requested an independent evaluation from the school on their youngest son's reading skills, Dale Botting says, "We were told we were Type A parents." Tests by a commercial tutoring firm later showed their son lagged behind others of his age in his reading ability. The following year, when the Bottings returned to Saskatchewan, school officials in Regina concluded their son was six months behind Grade 2 reading levels, despite the extra tutoring. He has since caught up to his peers and is doing well.

In Regina, the Bottings continued to ask pointed questions about education. Though more satisfied with education in Saskatchewan than in Ontario, the Bottings still wanted information about the content of their children's education. They were uneasy about the "spiral curriculum," which repeats material learned in earlier grades, the practice of showing commercial movies in classroom time (before Christmas it was *Beethoven*, about the misadventures of a St. Bernard) and questionable field trips to fast-food outlets. "Our kids are in school to learn, not to watch movies," declares Dale Botting.

The difficulty in obtaining direct, clear and informative answers from schools has a familiar ring. But it is too easy to blame the schools. When Dale Botting joined a local parent advisory council in Regina to talk about educational objectives, for example, he encountered strong resistance from other parents. "I was told, 'We don't talk about those sorts of things here,'" he says ruefully. Now, as a business representative on a Saskatchewan government review committee on education, Botting is hopeful he can get a clearer picture of what the schools are really trying to do.

As the Bottings' story illustrates, concerned parents want credible information about their children's schooling. They want to get beyond the rhetoric of "excellence" and "equity" and find out what it is that their children should know and when they should know it. Finally, they want to know how well students have learned the material they were taught. These questions trigger intense, ideological disagreements because they focus on differing ideas about the essence of education and on whose vision of education will prevail.

By a "vision of education" we mean an overall description of the essential purposes of elementary and secondary education. This should be set in a coherent view of the social, economic and moral context of school and include a clear statement of exactly what is expected of the student at each stage of the process. Such a statement of objectives should list not only required knowledge and skills but the competencies our children will need as responsible citizens in the coming decades.

"Why," one may wonder, "do we need another statement of philosophy, another set of goals, another vision?" After all, provincial education authorities have always had statements of their "goals of education." Indeed they have, but the point is: *They have never made any difference* because they are disconnected from the everyday reality of schools and their communities. Few teachers or school administrators could ever recall any of the provincial goals of education; there are no consequences for students for not achieving them; and no school programs are ever assessed on the basis of making provision for the official goals.

The three tests of a reinvented education system, we argue, are clarity, integrity and accountability. Most provincial statements of visions and goals — even including the latest one issued by Ontario in February 1993[1] — fail one or more of these tests. As lofty philosophical declarations, they are open to subjective interpretation.

They fail to address the new realities Canadians face in the work-place and in the world. Finally, they fail to provide for adequate measurement of performance.

Education has lost its way, in no small part because of lack of clarity over what students should know in order to prepare themselves for an uncertain and troubled world; for example, we know that many of the jobs in the twenty-first century do not yet exist and will literally be invented by young people now in school. Yet schools make little provision for students to acquire the entrepreneurial attitudes and skills required for that kind of world. The expectation remains that most graduates will find employment with large companies or in the public sector.

Without a consensus on the nature and purpose of education, neither the providers nor the consumers of education can make much progress. Educators cannot plan new curricula or instructional strategies and parents and employers cannot find out what should be the result of the education process. Competing interest groups have their own views about what should be added to the curriculum and those with enough political clout are often successful in getting their way. At the same time, the educational establishment retains its traditionally powerful role in developing new programs.

Developing a clear and shared sense of what should be expected of Canada's schools is a critical part of the public's taking back responsibility for their stewardship, instead of leaving it to the educational establishment. It is a process that must involve Canadians throughout this country at all levels — school, province and nation. It must take place in the context of a renewed commitment by all participants to play their part in translating expectations into reality. Finally, there must be support systems — for students, for schools and for school systems — to ensure that all of them live up to expectations.

Right now, there is no mandate, no forum and no political context for such deliberations. The federal government's "prosperity" initiative with its wish list of educational changes took place in a political vacuum; Ottawa lacked the mandate and provincial governments lacked the commitment to effect the proposed reforms. A number of provinces have undertaken major reviews of their school systems but have failed to set their individual school systems in the broader national and global contexts in which today's children are now growing up. Moreover, there is little evidence that these revamped provincial philosophies of education meet the final test of accountability: public confidence that students and schools are meeting the goals set for them.

In sorting out what is essential for ensuring excellence for all students from what is not — the essence of a clear vision for education — Canadians need to reconsider some of the assumptions around which the programs and expectations of schools are presently built. Just as changes are needed in the structure and decision-making framework for schools, and just as schools must redefine the ways they go about their work, so too assumptions about the appropriate form of the school curriculum need to be re-examined.

Curriculum as the Outcome of Schooling

Traditionally, curriculum development is treated as one of the prime "inputs" in the education process. Ministry-approved curriculum guidelines, textbooks and other authorized materials set the context for what happens in classrooms throughout each province. The central bureaucracies, and in some cases the local school boards, select or write course material for individual teachers who then adapt it for use in their classrooms. In effect, the education bureaucracies play a central role in determining what knowledge is most important in every student's school experience. For their part, teachers are expected to show that they and the students have covered the material mandated by the provincial curriculum.

Historically, though, schools and the public have paid much less attention to the results of education. What knowledge and skills, for example, must students demonstrate to advance to the next stage of their academic experience? What safeguards exist to ensure that students actually master some core body of knowledge, skills and attitudes? Who is responsible for determining if students can demonstrate competency in the fundamental building blocks of a strong education? In some provinces, ministry-composed tests and exams measure student knowledge of material deemed to be important. Elsewhere, student learning is assessed simply by the classroom teacher.

One of the characteristics of the new paradigm for education is a strong commitment to defining the entire package of knowledge, skills and attitudes that students should acquire as a result of their educational experience. Just as success in school depends on a shift in focus from teaching to learning, a shift in emphasis is needed to make stronger connections between curriculum inputs and outcomes, namely what is actually achieved. Clear statements of provincial or national standards — negotiated by all the stakeholders in education — will clarify what is expected of schools, leaving them free to modify the inputs to reach the desired goals. Such a model is consistent with a diminished role for the central bureaucracy and increased accountability of schools.

By keeping a closer watch on whether students achieve what is expected of them, schools will have more flexibility to determine how they deliver programs. With time as the variable and learning the constant, schools will be in a better position to ensure that students actually master the material and show competency in both basic and higher-order skills. For its part, the public can keep a close watch, too, lending support to an exercise for which it is responsible as well. The setting of well-defined standards — with adequate tools to measure the results — is essential to giving meaning to the notion of education based on outcomes.

The reorientation to what actually occurs as a result of the school experience is part of a worldwide phenomenon in education. In the United States, several states have revamped their education systems to sharpen the focus on results. One of the leaders of this movement is Kentucky, an economically depressed state determined to improve its economic opportunities with a better-educated population. The Kentucky Education Reform Act of 1990 establishes performance outcomes for all students, a key provision of the legislation. "Teachers, school administrators and school board members will be held accountable for helping students meet the student performance outcomes."[2] The state sets specific goals for schools, including higher rates of student retention, lower drop-out rates and higher expectations for all students. Moreover, schools are measured on the proportion of students who make a successful transition to work, post-secondary education and the military. School districts with more than 5 per cent drop-outs and fewer than 75.4 per cent of students making a successful transition from high school have to develop school improvement plans to demonstrate their accountability.

On the basis of the state's educational goals, the Council on School Performance Standards, a Kentucky state agency, developed seventy-five "outcomes" such as basic communication and mathematics skills; core concepts in science, math and the humanities; and thinking and problem-solving skills. Students in Grades 4, 8 and

12 will be tested annually using paper and pencil tests, in addition to new "performance-based" assessments, such as samples of student work and the performance of tasks that require students to solve problems. Kentucky is moving to new kinds of evaluation because they paint a broader picture of student ability than is possible from standardized tests.

In Canada, a number of provinces also are moving to embrace curriculum reforms that define expectations of student achievement. Nova Scotia, for example, has adopted "essential learning goals" reminiscent of those adopted in Kentucky. Nova Scotia's goals for students include effective communication, math literacy, problem solving, personal and social skills, critical and creative thinking, technology literacy and independent learning. In Alberta, under the rubric of "results-based" curriculum, the province promises high standards of what students are expected to know and to be able to do. The curriculum will also emphasize basic skills in verbal and written communication and math.

In British Columbia, where major education reforms are midway through completion, the government has gone further than most other provinces in looking at curriculum and assessment changes from the learner's point of view. The curriculum allows for "continuous learning" so that students progress at their own rate without being bound by the definition of traditional grades. As a result, a student may move through the material more quickly or more slowly than his or her classmates. Like other provinces, British Columbia is developing statements of student achievement — known as "reference sets" — so that students, parents and the public know what progress should be expected through school. Like other Canadian provinces, and Kentucky, British Columbia is experimenting with new forms of assessment based on what the learner actually does, for example, using for assessment a portfolio of written work through the school year, instead of relying exclusively on standardized tests that give a limited one-time snapshot.

In Ontario, where public dissatisfaction is particularly intense, the ministry of education also purports to be making curriculum reforms tied to what is actually achieved in the students' school experience. To that end, the ministry has devised for all students through Grade 9 a "common curriculum," defined in terms of intended learning outcomes. Using the same kind of "eduspeak" that is common to most provinces but that baffles the public, the ministry describes "ten essential cross-curricular learning outcomes" that must underlie all school programs and activities";[3] for example, students will learn to communicate effectively, apply standards of aesthetic value to work and entertainment and employ mathematical skills to solve practical problems.

However, there are dangers that "outcomes-based education" could be just another fad. Unlike British Columbia, which brought in its still-controversial reforms on the basis of a royal commission on education in the late 1980s, Ontario has no political mandate for change in education. The policy flip-flops over the past year come as the government, sensing the public's darkening mood, tries to get ahead of the curve. But those on the receiving end of the new curriculum proposals, including parents, students, teachers and employers, are disgruntled they have not been consulted in a meaningful way. Once again, the public perception is that the education insiders — ministry and school board bureaucrats — are imposing their philosophies on the system. At best, outcomes-based education holds potential to clarify expectations for students and schools. But in the absence of convincing explanations about the implications of a major reorientation of the curriculum, the public will be understandably suspicious that students are being used as guinea pigs in a new education gimmick that, like others before it, will pass in time.

Ontario has not helped its case for outcomes-based education by leaving doubts about how the public is supposed to evaluate whether the curriculum goals have been met. The government has promised to introduce a new program of evaluation, known as "benchmarks," to help parents and teachers discuss a student's progress toward meeting the stated outcome. One of the flaws of the benchmarks program, as currently defined, is that the standards are written in subjective terms that are open to interpretation; for example, "all students will use appropriate methods of computation" to demonstrate a thorough knowledge of arithmetic facts and mental calculation skills.

Another flaw in the approach is that there is no systematic assessment of all students — teachers would use the benchmarks at their discretion. The government's promise to turn the controversial issue of testing and assessment over to a commission of inquiry — a recognition of the need to develop a political consensus — now raises doubts as to the status of the benchmarks program. The commission, for example, could recommend a new approach to testing that makes the benchmarks project redundant before it sees the light of day.

Another risk of outcomes-based education is that it fails to build a solid foundation of what students are expected to know and be able to do. In Ontario, for example, one of the four new pillars of the "common curriculum" is "self and society," with students expected to "visualize and evaluate possible futures for themselves and their world" by the end of Grade 9. Such a statement is open to wide interpretation by school boards, which are responsible for translating the guidelines into new course content. Worse still, the statement gives students and parents no clue as to what content is to be acquired and mastered, adding to public cynicism that "learning outcomes" are just another means of obscuring what goes on at school.

The lack of rock-solid curriculum outcomes with objective measures, in Ontario as elsewhere, threatens to debase the currency of outcomes-based education. Pity the teacher who must develop course material on the basis of mushy outcomes instead of specific, measurable goals. In Ontario, well before the latest ministry moves, several of the large school boards had begun to develop their own statements of expected student achievement. Many of these, however, are still too vague, too subjective or too filled with educational jargon to create the clear picture rightfully demanded by parents and others. And here, too, it is not clear what are the consequences for not meeting the stated goals.

Curriculum as Maximum or Minimum Expectations

There are always new and legitimate demands that put pressure on the school curriculum. One significant source of external pressure on the education system is the explosion of new information. Scientific knowledge doubled in the 200 years between 1740 and 1940, but it doubled again in only twenty years between 1940 and 1960.[4] For today's young people, exposed from an early age to the latest technology, the sheer volume of data competing for their attention leaves the designers of curriculum scrambling to be relevant and timely. Those expected to stir the imagination of a generation raised on Nintendo and television are themselves apprehensive about and uncomfortable with computers and the new technology of learning. In the face of this knowledge revolution, Thomas Huxley's question "What knowledge is of most worth?" is even more pointed today than when it was posed 100 years ago.

Yet another source of external pressure is rising public expectations. Parents, employers and governments demand that schools provide the depth and breadth of curriculum and support services necessary to keep an increasingly diverse range of students in school through graduation. At the same time, the public is increasingly critical of schools for not providing "value for money." Though spending on education has risen dramatically over the past twenty years, the functional literacy of Canadians has shown little or no improvement. Citing Statistics Canada and other sources, the Economic Council of Canada in its 1992 report on education and training concludes: "Educational success in fostering cognitive achievement has stagnated, at best, over the last two or three decades and...it may, in fact, have declined."[5]

Yet one may pick up any school information brochure and a tempting menu of courses pours out like fruit from a cornucopia. From traditional subject disciplines to new interdisciplinary courses, the school calendar mirrors the escalating demands of society for choice, variety and options. The trouble is, schools are left promising more than they can deliver given the limitations on time and budget. The diverse social needs of the student population, the inclusion of students of widely varied ability in the same classroom and the sheer volume of material teachers are supposed to cover raise legitimate questions about how schools can deliver a quality service. As a result, provincial curricula look like a bureaucrat's dream of the most any student can achieve in a year, instead of the minimum standards required of all students.

These curriculum pressures have led some to call for a return to "the basics." But here again there is controversy. At its most passionate, the struggle pits the so-called "old basics" against the "new basics." Some grassroots parents' groups, for example, complain that schools have wandered far from their academic mandate and that they fail to teach the fundamentals of reading, writing and arithmetic. For these critics, the remedy is a return to traditional methods, including direct teacher instruction, spelling by phonics, drill work and standardized external exams. From this point of view, the school curriculum should be overhauled to deliver more meat and less mush. By contrast, business groups argue that more innovative approaches to teaching and learning are essential to equip young people with the skills now demanded by the new economy. If the "old basics" emphasized read, remember and regurgitate, the "new basics" require students to think, solve problems and work in teams.

The lack of clarity over curriculum expectations has several repercussions. Students receive mixed signals about academic standards, knowing that the full range of material cannot be mastered during the year. Teachers have to make choices about what should be in the course, often with little guidance or a publicly agreed sense of what is most important to the success of the student. In a study of provincial science curricula in 1984, the now-defunct Science Council of Canada concluded that what was actually taught was a pale shadow of the intended course content.[6] Ann Jones, superintendent of curriculum services for the Ottawa Board of Education, says the education professionals are caught between the conflicting demands of parents and business people. "These two warring factions continue to keep the education system in limbo," says Jones, a former math teacher and a strong advocate of the move to define what is expected as a result of the school experience. "One group which wants a classical education says, 'Give me what I knew — rote learning, phonetic spelling, the multiplication tables.' On the other side, employers are looking for the new basics — computer literacy, group work, flexible thinkers." How can we expect academic excellence from the schools when our expectations are so many, so diverse and virtually impossible to achieve?

Setting unrealistic expectations for the curriculum means that it is difficult to develop fair, objective assessments of student achievement. Without a solid sense of what is essential for all students in a course or program, it is difficult for the public to know whether students have learned the material or not. Province-wide tests for students in their final year of high school, where they exist, provide one form of check on classroom instruction. But the link between the intended curriculum, as specified in ministry guidelines, and what is actually taught can be broken in a couple of ways. Faced with a crowded curriculum, a teacher will teach material likely to appear on the test. Alternatively, without province-wide testing, teachers may select only the elements of the intended curriculum that they think are important. Either way, students are shortchanged in their educational experience.

A reinvented education system, by contrast, shifts the focus from maximum to minimum expectations for the curriculum. The new guideposts of a reorganized curriculum would set objectively measurable minimum standards for what all students must learn and be able to do. They may not learn all the material at the same speed, but, in the end, they must demonstrate that they have grasped concepts and skills required for a well-rounded education. At present, though, schools do both too much and too little about the enterprise of learning. By trying to be all things to all people, they create unrealistic expectations in the minds of students and the public. At the same time, schools do too little to guarantee that students actually achieve basic competency in the fundamentals of communication and mathematics. Too often, students who fail to accomplish basic skills are promoted to the next grade on the theory that they should move along with their peers. Although these students may maintain their self-esteem at least in the short run, they are sure to lose it in the long run if they are without the building blocks needed to master new material. In the confusion over curriculum, teachers, students and parents play out their roles as adversaries, not allies, in an exercise in which no one is held accountable for defining and delivering results. Teachers and school officials privately acknowledge they need to strike a better balance between the social objectives of school, such as self-esteem, and the academic goals of excellence built on attaining one standard before moving on to the next.

Education professionals and the public need to explore what are their minimum (but not low) expectations for the curriculum. By setting solid, achievable goals, schools and society at large will clarify, for parents and students alike, what every student should know and be able to do. By paring down grandiose promises to ensure that all students master a certain core of knowledge and skills, schools can be held to account in a more realistic fashion. In helping to define minimum standards, the public will have to take some responsibility to assist schools and students to meet the new goals. In the current environment, there are few links made between expectations and outcomes in education, so that no one is held personally accountable for results. Students are not held to a high standard of personal best. Parents are not called to account when they fail to create a home environment that supports high achievement in their children's endeavour. Teachers are not held accountable if they fail to reach all members of the class.

Minimum standards are not low standards. There is a world of difference between an objective that is realistically set and that everyone is expected to meet (such as in a driver's test) and a standard that may be high but that is met by only a few. Our expectations for student achievement can surely be raised in every province but on terms that are realistic and achievable.

The promise of outcomes-based education with its commitment to improving results will be empty if the message does not get through to the classroom level. At the start of every school year, students should know what goals to shoot for and indeed be part of the exercise of defining them. They should know too what are the consequences of not achieving their best. Students, teachers, schools and the community at large must join forces to ensure that their school meets all the minimum objectives of the curriculum. There should be rewards for those who do even better.

The Battle over Process and Content

Education suffers from fads and gimmicks. As the pendulum swings from one extreme to another, ideas about teaching and learning fall in and out of favour. Teachers, parents and students are rightly sceptical when the experts embrace a new concept as the latest solution to today's education problems. One example of this phenomenon comes in the recent move to revamp the curriculum so that it emphasizes "process" — the how-we-know issues — at the expense of content — the what-we-know issues.

Traditionally, the curriculum has been designed so that students learn to accumulate — and spew back — a litany of facts. The ability to remember people, events and ideas in some logical sequence was the definition of academic prowess. Now, education professionals and others argue that what you know is less important than how you know it. To some degree, all the provinces are re-evaluating curriculum so that students learn how to find, synthesize and analyze information instead of being told by the teacher what to think and remember. The shift in emphasis is a corollary of the "new basics," in which narrow subject disciplines are merged into new cross-curricular courses that integrate themes and ideas. The principle is that students become "active" learners in that they generate their own ideas and projects instead of passively waiting for the teacher to impart information and provide the analysis.

With its education reforms, British Columbia is at the forefront of the move to emphasize process over content. Teachers at Delta Secondary School, outside Vancouver, are enthusiastic about the benefits of such a reorientation. "Rather than being passive recipients, students become active," says Gord Macdonald, co-operative education program director. "That can sometimes be seen as a threat to the traditional way things have been done in North America. But I think it is certainly worth the risks when you look at the incredible changes in technology that we are living through. What I am seeing is kids who have the ability to think and reason and develop creative strategies to solve difficult problems."

A practical example of the theory can be found in a data-processing course at the school; business studies students produce a profit-making school newspaper, generating ads from the local community. "The focus is on producing the product," says Macdonald, "but that can't be done unless the individual students have the basic skills. What I have seen in those classes is that the kids spend more time working on the content because they have to master it in order to do the project at hand."

Meanwhile, in a project funded by the provincial government, two Delta teachers have integrated math and science for Grade 8 students in an attempt to make the curriculum more relevant to students. "A lot of the students were finding that school math wasn't very relevant to their lives or they were only seeing it on paper rather than in real-life questions," says Janice Willcox, a biology teacher who worked with science department head Gary Storsley on the project. The students themselves, she says, view traditional subjects as unrelated to one another. "They come to class and say, 'This is science. We do this in math but we are not supposed to do that in science.' They attempt to keep the courses separate." In their project, the Delta teachers have developed a course that brings math concepts and the application of science to bear on a real-life issue. As part of their course, the students visited a nearby forest to collect data on species, with each team examining a square metre plot. For the science component, the students collected samples of species, comparing life in the forest to that found in a nearby meadow and creek. In math class, the students worked in pairs to calculate averages, means, and medians and to graph the class data. As part of the exercise, they learned about the collection of information and interpretation of data. "It was using a practical experience to bring across a mathematical concept," says Storsley, "and it was more relevant to them because they actually did the counting. It was their data and they really cared." Before and after their environmental project, the students were surveyed on their views about the relevance of math and science to daily life. "Afterwards they saw that math was something that they could be using in their life whereas, before, a lot of them saw it as a paper-and-pencil exercise," says Willcox.

If implemented well, curriculum changes that encourage students to make stronger connections between their world and the one they will join as adults hold out exciting possibilities. But the new focus comes at a price. The exercise is time-consuming and labour-intensive for teachers. Teachers have to work together in teams, class schedules have to be rearranged or even expanded to accommodate projects and more preparation time is required to ensure the material is covered well. In a fiscal environment of budget cutbacks and teacher lay-offs, such modifications are easier talked about than done.

Ann Jones of the Ottawa board says a successful shift in curriculum depends on well-trained teachers and parents' understanding that structure and content have not been jettisoned in the name of yet another education fad. "We need to say to our parents, 'Look, I am not letting go of the learning outcomes. I am going to plan carefully enough that you understand that when you look in my classroom and you see all these kids working with the stock market game [an integrated learning project] and adding up things and using calculators, and in their costumes being Madame Somebody's Cosmetic Company, that counts as learning, and I am going to test the outcomes.'" The trouble is that the public has lost confidence in the willingness of education experts and the school bureaucracies to experiment with new ideas without a guarantee of good results. Many parents find it hard to get the kind of straight answers that Jones says the system must give to parents, students and the public.

The level of suspicion that subject matter content is being downgraded runs especially high in Ontario, where successive governments have tried to implement curriculum reforms over the last ten years. The lack of specific content in key ministry policy documents meant that some subjects, such as science, were sometimes omitted altogether in the junior grades, as the Science Council of Canada discovered in its 1984 study of science education. Finally, in 1986, in response to public criticism, the ministry issued a policy statement requiring all schools to provide specific science programs. Form without content is of little value even when constructing courses to deliver the "new basics." Students need to learn subjects well and, in turn, learn how to integrate ideas and concepts from various subjects together.

On philosophical grounds, there is cause to be sceptical of curriculum reforms that put a premium on learning how to learn at the expense of a core body of knowledge. University of Western Ontario professors Robin Barrows and John McPeck argue that learning to think and analyze does not occur in isolation.[7] Thinking processes are significantly different depending on the subject at hand. One's ability to think creatively in music, for example, is quite different from the creativity required to analyze a piece of literature or to design a scientific experiment. One may well ask if "creativity" in a generic or content-free sense means anything at all. Charles Ungerleider, director of field placement and research at the Faculty of Education at the University of British Columbia, worries that the pendulum has swung too far at the expense of content. "Critical thinking does not happen in a vacuum. In order to think critically, you need something to think critically about," he declares. To be sure, teachers need to explore new opportunities to encourage students to be observant and thoughtful about issues, but the exercise will not be successful without well-structured and content-filled courses of study.[8]

Like the unproductive debate over the "new basics" and the "old basics," the conflict between process and content is not an "either-or" situation. Schools do need to ensure that students are equipped with a broad range of skills and abilities but these skills must be set in a strong context of subject matter content. The curriculum needs to provide a judicious blend of subject disciplines and process, and it should be articulated as clearly as possible for all to understand. Vague curriculum goals serve no one well.

Can Schools Solve Society's Problems?

The lack of a clear and unified vision of the mission of schools is rooted in broader confusion over how public education should respond to a changing environment. Aside from their academic and vocational obligations, schools are vehicles for imparting acceptable social habits, attitudes and values. In an increasingly diverse society, with varying cultural, social and political values, the challenge is to find the common thread that binds people together. In another respect, schools are a means of preparing students for citizenship in a democratic society. "We can think of the public education system as the mechanism for ensuring that there is a society," says Ungerleider. "I don't think that in a modern, heterogeneous, primarily urban society, you can achieve community without an institution like the public school." At issue, though, is how large a role schools should play in forming the moral character of society.

Some see public education as a tool of economic renewal. Every interest group, government report and business leader has a shopping list of what schools should teach to meet the demands of the next century. The growing interest of the business community in education is motivated, in part, by concerns that schools are not graduating the quality of worker needed for tomorrow's economy. School reforms in New Brunswick, for example, are predicated on the assumption that a better educated and trained workforce will ensure the province's transformation from a have-not to a have province.

In other quarters, schools are seen as a means of social reform. Schools, it is felt, should do more than mirror society; they should improve its quality of life. Faced with an array of social, economic and political problems, society looks to schools as the cure-all for its ills. In response to growing interest in the environment, for example, schools add environmental education to the curriculum. In response to racist incidents, schools introduce anti-racist education. The growth in school-supported "heritage" language programs is a reaction to growing demands from ethnic and racial minorities to be represented in the curriculum. Global education is the latest curriculum innovation, a response to the changing world economic and political order. Meanwhile, in recognition of the damage done by illegal drug use and sexually transmitted diseases, schools have expanded their commitments to teach about personal health and responsibility.

In the current environment, in which school time remains constant and resources are declining, schools cannot do it all. Something in the curriculum has to give, but there is no public forum that can decide what is most worth learning or what are the limits of what schools can and ought to achieve. Instead, schools try to cover all the bases, with a nod in the direction of the political, social and economic goals of education. Like society's other institutions, schools are imperfect. Those imperfections are magnified when schools are expected to serve as surrogate parents, social workers and religious leaders. Clarifying the vision of the schools' central mission requires both the users and providers of the education service to distinguish between the primary and secondary objectives of school. The primary mandate of schools is to teach — and of students to learn — the knowledge and skills that will ensure they mature as democratic citizens in an uncertain world.

The point is not that schools avoid teaching religious and racial tolerance; instead, the challenge is to teach values as a corollary to the main mission of schools, not as another add-on that should be given equal weight in the curriculum. In the end, every component of the school's mandate should be examined through a single prism: What's most worth learning?

Standards for a New Age

Education's lack of clear goals has eroded public confidence in the overall enterprise. Canadians need to reach a new consensus on what they expect of schools and how to gauge whether the results have been achieved. Furthermore, some standards need to be set out at the national level rather than separately for each province. Not only will this ease mobility and transferability of educational qualifications; it will encourage the participation of all sectors of society in a task that to a great extent defines who we are as a nation. This need not conflict in any way with the present constitutional position with respect to provincial jurisdiction over schooling. While the provincial governments are still the most appropriate ones to operate and fund school systems, it does not follow that the overall standards also must be set provincially.[9]

We propose the establishment of a Canadian Educational Standards Council (CESC), a body representing the broad spectrum of stakeholders in elementary and secondary education in Canada, with the mandate to set national standards for each level of educational achievement. This council would be funded and appointed by federal and provincial governments but operate at arm's length from both of them. It would include members of the business and academic communities as well as representatives of all aspects of Canadian society.[10] The council would have a small expert staff to enable it to fulfil its mandate and the resources to conduct studies concerning standards in other jurisdictions. It would operate in close collaboration with another national agency, which should be established to conduct educational testing and assessments. The council would report both to Parliament and to the Council of Ministers of Education, the body that represents the provinces and territories, and would publish its findings for all Canadians.

What is important is to begin, at long last, the journey to defining what Canadians expect of their schools. "We need a national forum for discussion of educational issues," says Veronica Lacey, director of education for North York, who endorses national standards and testing. "We must be the only country in the world that can't get its act together as a nation to talk about educational issues."

Under such an arrangement, provinces would be free to adopt the recommended national standards for the schools within their jurisdiction or be held accountable to their electorate for failing to do so. The proposed council would not define 100 per cent of the school curriculum but rather determine the minimum standards in core areas of the curriculum — language, math, science, social studies and the arts at key stages of school, such as at Grades 3, 6, 9 and high school graduation. Provinces could choose to add specific requirements or expectations that would apply to their own jurisdiction.

Establishing the Canadian Educational Standards Council would demonstrate that Canadians are prepared to put the politics of blame behind them in order to take responsibility for their schools. As a result, schools throughout Canada would then have a set of uniform, clear and measurable goals to use as the basis for program planning. The role of each community school council (with representation of the teachers in each school) would be to determine school curricula and teaching strategies that respond both to the national standards and to the distinct social context of their own school population. National standards would not be so onerous that their achievement would consume all the time and energy of students and teachers. Rather, teachers would be able to use additional time to enrich the school experience in ways that reflect local interests and needs; for example, one school might focus on science and technology, while another would emphasize Oriental language and culture. In any case, teachers would have the freedom they need to assist those needing extra time to reach the basic standards. While there could be many differences among some schools, the national standards would define the common core expected of all schools.

Parents and families would then know, unequivocally, what to expect of their school regardless of its location in Canada. Students moving from one community to another would encounter different curricula, new textbooks and a variety of teaching methods, within the context of common core program goals. Employers would know that a graduate from any high school in Canada could be expected to demonstrate competency in certain well-defined common skills. Taxpayers would know that their community school could be assessed on the basis of its results, year after year, on national competency tests as well as on its own unique program. Publishers and other private-sector suppliers to the education system would have a single set of standards for which to prepare materials, the larger, national market resulting in a richer array of curriculum materials for schools than is now possible. Teachers and other school professionals could move from school to school, from province to province, far more easily than is now the case, knowing that the requirements of every school are based on one and the same national standards.

What has prevented the move to national standards in the past? In a word, politics. The provinces have long resisted any suggestion of federal involvement in educational affairs. The provinces have a poor track record of co-operation with each other on education and training issues. The Council of Ministers of Education, which represents the ten provinces and two territories on issues from kindergarten to university, is a politically weak body that has made few contributions to the education debate in Canada. The high turnover of ministers of education and the requirement of consensus thwart the building of political momentum, even when they might agree to act in concert.

However, times are changing in ways that hold out the potential for a political breakthrough on the issue of national standards. Ground-breaking work is in progress to develop national standards for the training of technologists, an exercise that grows out of the close co-operation among industry, community colleges and the professionals themselves.[11] To their credit, the federal government and several provinces have expressed their strong support for an exercise in educational nation building that is long overdue.

The creation of national standards would allow, for the first time in Canada, for a national forum for effective deliberations over the purpose and content of education. If led responsibly, such discussions would form the basis for a truly defensible national curriculum, which would respect and preserve the provinces' traditional jurisdiction over education. This is a compromise that has eluded Canadians for over a century. But, given the general level of public anxiety about the future, the proposed compromise must now be pursued with vigour and dispatch. The answer to "What knowledge is of most worth?" will always be a political compromise, one that evolves to meet changing circumstances and priorities. To be sure, the effort will produce both good and bad compromises, all part of taking responsibility for Canada's schools. But reforming the means for determining the educational future of our children must be a national priority.

Chapter 6

Measuring Success

*T*esting *is a* significant barometer of public concern over education. As discontent rises over the state of schools, the system is under more pressure to demonstrate improvements. The storm warnings come from all segments of society. Parents, business and taxpayers have their own agendas on issues of student achievement but they share a common desire for reliable evidence that the system is delivering results. At a time when Canada spends proportionately more than most other industrial countries on education, the critics need only cite the mediocre showing of Canadian students on recent international tests as evidence that all is not right. The reluctance of most ministry and school board bureaucracies to publish data on student and school performance fuels latent public fears about declining quality. The staunch opposition of some teachers' groups to certain kinds of testing leaves the impression that they and the rest of the education establishment have something to hide.

Conflict over testing contributes to the general level of discord in education. As in other aspects of the debate, there are disagreements over the most basic issues, such as the purposes and goals of testing. Too often, testing is viewed as an end in itself, as if rankings in international comparisons of student achievement were the point of the exercise. Despite the media's tendency to treat it this way, testing is too important an issue to be treated as an Olympic sporting event. Testing is always a means to an end, with the results being used as feedback to decisions about some aspect of the educational process: the diagnosis of individual student problems; the need to improve course content or modify teaching methods; the readiness of a student to move into a new program; the adequacy of provincial standards in a subject area and so on.

Testing is also an issue of political control. In other words, who is best situated to judge a student's learning — the classroom teacher or those removed from the classroom? The conflict plays out in the debate over what is worth learning — "But teacher," the student asks, "will it be on the test?" — and over the best forms of evaluation to paint a complete picture of student achievement. All these conflicts, and more, escalate to new heights when the public already is anxious about the threat of Canada losing ground economically. Amid these concerns, the education system faces rising public expectations for schools to deliver excellence for all students. At issue is what role testing should play in meeting that objective.

Compounding these conflicts is the fact that valid and reliable testing is a technically complex business in which even teachers are rarely well trained. And as with most technically complex fields, testing has accumulated its own share of jargon. Thus when the public expects straight answers, educators (most with only a partial understanding themselves of the technical language of testing) too often resort to *eduspeak* (see box); for example, some members of the educational community use the term "continuous learning" as a code phrase for the philosophy that students not be allowed to fail. "Authentic assessment" is jargon for reviewing what students actually produce during the year, including essays and projects, that illustrates their progress over time. There is a world of difference between an educational "standard" and "standardized" testing (see box) — a distinction lost on the public because the experts do such a poor job of explaining both the terminology and its implications. Hiding behind jargon that few people understand, the educational establishment reinforces a climate of mistrust and suspicion.

Eduspeak

The jargon of the educational establishment is one of the biggest impediments to well-informed public debate. Decoding the eduspeak of testing is the first step towards making informed decisions about the issues. Some analogies may help in deciphering the language of testing.

Criterion-Referenced Test: The Driving Test

Most adults remember the terror (or joy) of taking a provincial drivers' test. One had to meet pre-determined standards to demonstrate driving competence. Individual performance was judged against absolute standards, not by comparison with other drivers. In the same way, criterion-referenced tests measure a student's achievement against certain educational standards or objectives, such as writing a paragraph free of spelling mistakes. For testing experts, criterion-referenced tests are

---

increasingly attractive tools because they measure student performance against an external standard.

Norm-Referenced Test: The World Series

In the final days of the baseball or hockey season, fans are eager to know where their favourite team stands in relation to others in the division or the league. Thus, the team's winning percentage is less significant than its lead over the nearest rival. In the same way, norm-referenced tests measure a student's relative position in the class or in some larger group. As a result, student marks are adjusted to fit a predetermined notion of the "normal" distribution of As to Fs, a practice known as "marking to the curve." Norm-referenced tests are less popular for educational purposes today because they do not paint an accurate picture of individual student achievement.

Standard and Standardized Tests

Some tests are used year after year with similar groups of people — those used as admission tests to law school or medical school, for example. These tests have been "standardized" in that the marks from a very large number of students have been related statistically to one another. In some cases, the results of students in one year may be compared with a statistically "normal" distribution from previous years, creating a type of norm-referenced test. Most lay people use the term "standardized" more loosely than this, referring to any kind of multiple-choice or computer-marked test.

By contrast, other tests are written by all students in a particular group, say all Grade 10 students in Alberta. Everyone in the group answers the same questions at the same time in a prescribed time period. The test can be called "standard" in that it is related to the curriculum taught to all students. It is also a standard because all students take the same test. It is a criterion-referenced test, however, and the marks should not be statistically related to any predetermined pattern. This test is thus not a "standardized" test.

The need for more *standardized* testing in education is actually very limited. By contrast, *standard* testing conducted nationwide and based on nationally agreed goals is both necessary and desirable.

Public unhappiness over the absence of clear, objective measures of student achievement takes many forms. All parents want clarity, namely an honest and understandable appraisal from teachers about students' progress. They also want integrity. That is, assessments should be based on a real standard and students' progress towards that standard should be accurately determined. For example, universities and colleges complain that high school marks have lost their meaning because some schools inflate the results for their graduates. An A given today might have rated only a B ten years ago when there was less pressure on students to compete for limited spaces at universities and community colleges. Some schools are more lenient than others in their grading system, creating more uncertainties about the meaning of marks. Many employers say they have lost confidence in the worth of a high school diploma, reciting horror stories of graduates unable to spell accurately or make the correct change. Finally, as taxpayers, citizens want accountability. Weary of the almost inexorable rise in education taxes, Canadians are looking for an education system that, for the large funds invested, yields correspondingly high dividends.

For some, the uncertain picture on student achievement sparks an understandable yearning for the apparent simplicity of "the good old days" when the situation seemed so much better. A return to traditional school exams at the end of high school, for example, is heralded as much-needed external evaluations required to push schools to new heights of accountability. However, nostalgia for the past overlooks the shortcomings of conventional testing methods, which assess only a narrow range of student achievement; for example, one of the objectives of all science programs is that students will develop skill in various "scientific processes" such as measurement. However, in a situation where the exam was simply a paper-and-pencil test, teachers and students would often overlook the practical aspects of the subject, knowing full well that those objectives would never be included in the assessment.

Indeed, the current furor over testing leaves the inaccurate impression that schools do little or no assessment. In reality, at almost every level of the system — from the classroom to the country as a whole — schools are engaged in an ever-widening array of testing activities. However, for the public, there is considerable confusion over what is going on because there is so little consistency from one school to the next. That lack of clarity feeds a natural tension between the public and the educational experts. The public, for the most part, exhibits a strong desire for simplicity while testing experts are busy designing ever more sophisticated evaluation practices. "People want simple answers to extremely complicated questions," says Douglas Hodgkinson, director of research and evaluation for the ministry of education in British Columbia. "It's very hard to describe where a student is in terms of performance. But everyone says, 'Give me a number, a figure, a letter, just tell me.'" Increasingly, school officials voice concern that the public demand for accountability will trigger an avalanche of testing that could overwhelm schools in meeting their obligations to bring about improvements for students.

At the provincial level, especially, there is more testing being undertaken than at any time in the past twenty years. After departmental examinations were abandoned in the late 1960s in many provinces, the political pendulum swung back in the direction of external measures of the system by the early 1980s, with almost all provinces now engaged in some form of systematic evaluation. Ontario, the largest province, has until very recently remained the strongest hold-out against external tests of students in their final year of high school. But recent signals from the new minister of education, Dave Cooke, suggest Ontario's resistance is breaking down. In British Columbia, Alberta, Québec and Newfoundland, students must write a province-wide exam to earn a portion (between 30 and 50 per cent) of their final grade for graduation. In Manitoba, students in their final year write one exam prepared by provincial testers.

Testing, of course, is expensive, especially the new methods of evaluation that focus on the individual performance of students in demonstrating their ability to think critically and solve problems. Such assessments are labour intensive, requiring people and not computers to do the marking. In an era of shrinking dollars for education, should Canadians spend more to bring in new, more sophisticated forms of testing and assessment? The short answer is yes. These new "performance-based" tests have a distinct advantage over traditional standardized tests in that they measure a wider spectrum of student achievement and, in the process, contribute to the individual's educational experience. Standardized tests are a relatively inexpensive way to measure a student's success in remembering facts, only one type of intellectual achievement. By contrast, performance tests attempt to measure a student's ability to reason well, the kind of skill now demanded by the business community.

The criteria for judging the merits of any test are whether it helps the student and whether it helps the system. Some kinds of tests are best suited for measuring individual performance; others are most appropriate for the system as a whole. Given the fiscal reality, the education community must engage the public in a discussion about the nature and purpose of testing and its contribution to quality and accountability. Parents, employers and others with a stake in education must play their part to sort out what is reasonable — and unreasonable — to expect from testing. Last but not least, students need to know how to make the most of testing and assessment for their own success at school. At the moment, the various interest groups are talking past one another on testing, unable to make the necessary connections between assessment and an effective school system.

Why Test?

Testing is only one facet of a publicly responsive education system. The hallmarks of a truly democratic educational system — clarity, integrity and accountability — apply to testing and assessment. Those who use the education service need reliable information with which to make informed decisions. Students need to know where they stand to develop a sense of their own strengths and weaknesses and to make sensible career choices. Parents want information that helps in monitoring their children's progress. Universities and colleges need consistent measures to make better decisions about admissions. Employers need to know that a high school transcript serves as a passport to competency in the workforce.

On their own, tests are not enough, as the U.S. experience amply demonstrates. By any yardstick, the United States is the most prolific country in the world when it comes to testing students. Yet the proliferation of standardized tests over the past decade has not led to notable improvements in education quality. Just as taking an X-ray will not mend a patient's broken arm, so testing is only one indicator of a student's academic health. The more important question is how the results are interpreted to improve individual learning and the system as a whole, goals to which all classroom teachers would surely subscribe. Within the classroom, teachers have an array of tools to evaluate student performance and make judgements about the need for remediation, for example. The classroom assessment, however essential, is only one part of the picture.

Predictive Testing

Some tests probe a student's likely success at some future task or course of study. The U.S. Scholastic Aptitude Test (SAT), for example, is a good predictor of success at the undergraduate level, enabling colleges and universities to weed out those lacking certain aptitudes and skills. Similarly, schools of medicine, law and graduate studies rely on their respective MSAT, LSAT and GSAT to screen out those least likely to succeed. These tests are standardized and norm-referenced because their predictive value is based on statistical correlations over time involving a large number of test takers.

Predictive tests, used extensively by U.S. colleges and universities, have come under sharp criticism in recent years for their alleged social, cultural and racial bias. In theory, such tests are supposed to measure a student's basic scholastic aptitude. In practice, many students go to private "crammers" or purchase guides to improve their performance. As a result, U.S. colleges are beginning to attach less significance to SAT scores in making their admission decisions.

In Canada, universities and colleges look to high school grades instead of SAT-type tests to evaluate applicants.

In the school system, testing is used to generate distinct types of information: on individual students; on the school and its programs; and on the system as a whole. How testing meets the objectives of clarity, integrity and accountability is different in all three categories. Let's look at each in more detail.

Individual Students: "How's My Child Doing?"

Frustration with the testing and assessment of their children is voiced by parents from all sides. For some, the complaints centre on vague, subjectively written report cards. For others, it is the "don't worry" attitude of teachers, even in the face of poor student results. Still others rage about the defensive response of teachers when they are challenged to explain their evaluations. Most parents simply want to know on a regular basis how their children are progressing, but feel thwarted when they cannot get straight answers from the school. Even affluent, well-educated parents complain their voice is not heard, raising questions about the ability of parents with less clout, education and expertise to get the answers they need from their children's schools.

Clare Elwood is one of the foot-soldiers in the silent army of parents unhappy about the paucity of reliable information about their children's progress. "There would be far less screaming, angry hostile parents if we were informed in a better fashion," says Elwood, a university-educated professional in a well-to-do section of London, Ontario. The frustrations experienced by Elwood are typical of many parents. At the parent-teacher interview in the fall of 1992, she sought answers about her ten-year-old son's difficulties in spelling and reading. "I asked how Robert was doing. The teacher said, 'Oh, he's fine, no problem,'" she recounts. Determined to get a more revealing assessment, she finally received a list of frequently misspelled "monster" words for her son to practise at home. But the experience left Elwood dissatisfied with the teacher's resistance to engage in a straightforward discussion. "We're paying for them to communicate," says Elwood. "It should be part of their mandate."

The crux of the matter for most parents is "How's my child doing?" At the best of times, a thorough, accurate answer is not easy. Increasingly, the professionals look beyond the traditional standardized test — which focuses on what a student knows about a certain body of knowledge — to so-called "performance" evaluations such as written essays and lab work that measure an individual's ability to analyze concepts and to apply them to real-life problems. These thinking skills, now in demand by employers, are not easily measured by fill-in-the-blanks tests.

Teachers and parents at one Toronto school have attempted to resolve the inherent tension between testing for knowledge and testing for skills. At Rosedale Heights Secondary School, a test site for a number of innovations in education, teachers, parents and students have designed a new report card that gives a more revealing snapshot of achievement than is traditionally given on student assessment reports (see Figure 2). For each unit of a course, the teacher uses in-class tests and quizzes to evaluate what students have learned. In addition, the teacher grades the students on whether they complete projects on time and how well they work in teams. Students are scored on the knowledge and skills required for the unit; the results of these ongoing evaluations ultimately contribute to a final mark at the end of the course. The new approach means that students must do more than study hard for a mid-term test; they must show commitment and industry throughout the course.

Using a software program developed at the school, each teacher produces a two-page report card with all the data, including a breakdown on the value of each unit and end-of-term comments. Parents can visit the school at any time for an up-to-date portrait of the student's activities provided by the computerized records. Students can do the same at any time. In addition, students take part in a one-on-one meeting with the teacher during the fall term to discuss both parties' assessment of the student's work and goals for the year.

The innovations at Rosedale Heights show what is possible when all those with a stake in the student's success have an opportunity to engage in a candid discussion about what is important in student assessment. Regular classroom evaluation, based on criteria understood by all parties, contributes to ongoing dialogue among students, parents and teachers about what is being learned and accomplished in the classroom. Students who have done poorly on one unit of the course are given an opportunity to redo the work and get a better grade.

Figure 2: An Alternative Report Card

Student Record of Achievement Form
Rosedale Heights Secondary School
393-1580

| Teacher: | WONG | Student Name: | DOE, JANE | | Student No: | 999123 |

| Subject: | MATHEMATICS | Course Code: | MAT3W001 | Grade: | 76% | Absent: | 7 | Late: | |

Unit Titles	Unit Weightings			Student Grades		
	Unit Wt.	Work Skills Wt.	Kwldge Skills Wt.	Work Skills %	Kwldge Skills %	Unit %
Polynomials	10	3	7	88%	81%	83%
Powers & Roots	10	3	7	79%	75%	76%
Examination	15		15		72%	72%

Term 1 Comments	Term 2 Comments	Term 3 Comments
Excellent work!		

The most sophisticated testing program is a waste of time if the results are not communicated clearly to students and parents. Parents need accurate, informative descriptions of how their children are doing in the early grades, just as older students need an honest appraisal of their work. Too often, teachers are encouraged to be upbeat at the expense of being honest, hiding behind subjective language or computer-generated comments such as "Generally satisfactory for his age," "She makes a great effort" or, worst of all, "Very fair."

More is known nowadays about how to assess complex objectives, but it takes expertise, money and time to construct balanced, comprehensive tests; for example, in the field of second language learning, most courses nowadays include both written and oral comprehension and expression. Systematic assessment of students' progress is harder to plan and more time-consuming to administer than a test of verb conjugation. Yet more sophisticated forms of assessment are essential if the full range of education objectives is to be taken seriously.

Some classroom teachers still adjust student marks to produce a range of final marks deemed acceptable by the principal or school board. This is a gross misapplication of statistical procedures and has no place at the classroom level. Testing of curriculum material should be based on clearly stated criteria, consistently applied and openly defensible. If test instruments are fairly designed, students in the course should all be able to score an A or a D if that grade reflects how they actually performed. There should be no predetermined or "right" distribution of grades, though a classful of Ds would surely be cause for concern. The basis of assessment should be the actual progress of students towards the defined course objectives, not a relative comparison of students in the class.

In response to public demands for more information, many provinces are devising new measures that are supposed to spell out what students should know at key stages of elementary and secondary school. These standards of student achievement are known as "benchmarks" (Ontario), "reference sets" (British Columbia) and "exemplars" (Alberta). In these and other provinces, students are tested at the end of Grades 3, 6 and 9 to assess how (on average) they fare against an expected standard. Although these assessment techniques mark a valiant attempt to paint a more complete picture of student achievement, they suffer from being too subjective and lacking in precision.

Benchmark Programs

As an alternative to standardized testing, the Toronto Board of Education has developed its own system of evaluation, which it has called "benchmarks." Videotapes are used to illustrate the range of student achievement, from excellent to poor, compared to predetermined standards. At age ten, for example, 10 per cent of students are expected to solve a particular kind of math problem with ease, while 30 per cent will have some difficulties and another 10 per cent may not solve the problem at all. From these board-produced videos, teachers can relate their own students' performance to what is expected for all students in Toronto. Unlike standardized tests, the Toronto benchmarks are not given to all students at one time. Instead, the benchmarks are used as a tool to diagnose learning problems.

With such diagnostic testing, schools hope to give parents a better sense of where their children stand in relation to the "norm." The Toronto program, which has been sold to boards in the United States, does not indicate what students should know, only what they do know. Moreover, Toronto does not test all students, unlike the benchmarks project in the adjacent North York board. For these reasons, critics say the Toronto benchmark program is an inadequate tool of assessment. The term "benchmarks" is also used by the Ontario Ministry of Education, developing a program much like that in Toronto, and by other boards (such as Ottawa and North York) to describe a more systematic approach to assessment. All these "benchmark" projects share one common feature: The results are not used to determine whether a student graduates.

Why is the education community so nervous about testing and assessment? Some teachers' concerns are based on the deficiencies of past assessment techniques, which paint a partial picture of student ability. Many standard tests, for example, usually require a student to pick one of four possible answers, revealing nothing of the individual's ability to solve problems. Other objections are based on a concern that teachers will be forced to "teach to the test," thereby limiting the student's learning experience. Still others worry that standard tests simply teach some students to expect failure in school. Teacher objections to testing are also rooted in self-interest and the fear of criticism coming to rest on them for the deficiencies of the system as a whole. External measures of student performance might translate, ultimately, into an indicator of teacher effectiveness in the classroom.

Why is it so difficult for teachers to communicate honestly with parents and students? Mistrust is the root cause, says Ann Jones, superintendent of curriculum services at the Ottawa board of education, which has developed its own city-wide testing. "There is a total lack of trust. Good teachers look at a group of students and see all the possibilities in that group of students. They know that this child is having trouble with math and they know that this one might be having trouble with reading. And if they put these kids through a standard test, what we are going to find out is exactly what the teacher already knows. That's not an action that is going to help the teacher. That's an action that's going to help the politician, the journalist. And help them do what? Beat the teacher on the head." Jones is an advocate of tests that reveal, as much as possible, the range of a student's ability.

Some teachers base their objections on fundamental grounds of control: a philosophical belief that the teacher is the best judge of what happens in the classroom. From the point of view of many teachers, education is a process of growth and development unique to each child rather than a race to attain specific knowledge and skills common to all. For such teachers, testing is like digging up a living plant to see how it is growing and, as such, is not beneficial to the child.

One of the concerns about standard testing is the difficulty of making direct links between student achievement and teaching quality. Attempts to make fair and accurate comparisons are fraught with difficulty. The Ottawa public board conducts regular city-wide tests, rotating subjects and grade levels from year to year. The city's top academic school always ranks first, while vocational schools with a less academic orientation wind up on the bottom. In 1991, the board investigated the links between socio-demographic data and school results. By matching test scores to income data by postal codes in the city, board researchers discovered an absolute match between the two. "High economic standard, high results," says Jones, confirming what the researchers expected to find.

The message should serve as a warning to those who see standardized or even standard tests as a panacea for what ails the school system. "What we are measuring is what good students — who have academic success — can do," says Jones. "We are not measuring those things that students without that academic prowess can do."

Not surprisingly, she says, many teachers dislike standardized tests because they do not value all students. The conclusion should not be that such forms of testing and evaluation are invalid. Instead, parents and other members of the public must be clear about what testing can and cannot do well.

Teacher organizations have paid a high political price for their public opposition to testing. In the minds of the public, teachers object to all forms of testing, a mis-impression that flies in the face of widespread testing practices in the classroom. Nevertheless, the teaching profession finds itself politically isolated from the rest of society, which is looking for comprehensive and reliable information on school performance. Tough economic realities have persuaded Canadians that the apparent "laissez-faire" philosophy in education, which dates to the 1960s, should be supplanted by a more hard-nosed approach in the 1990s to specify learning goals and measure results. Whether teachers like it or not, the public demands more testing. The most important issue is not whether to test but what forms are most appropriate for students and the system.

Accountability: "How's My School Doing?"

The most important purpose of testing is to assist individual learners. But testing is also a way to monitor the quality of educational programs, teaching practices and the performance of the school itself. If external assessment of individual learning is currently inadequate, testing for quality control at the school level is almost non-existent in Canadian education. With some notable exceptions, most education authorities are reluctant to disseminate school test scores.

Advocates of standard testing argue that published results would enable parents to make more informed choices about where to send their children to school. At first glance, the logic is compelling. Schools with good results would attract more students and those with poorer results would lose support. As things stand, the absence of much comparative data leaves the public suspicious that Canadian schools and teachers can do better. If parents are to make intelligent choices for their children then they deserve clear unvarnished information about the implications. But simplistic school-to-school comparisons do no one any good. It is not just a matter of "weeding out" poor schools, as some in the United States have suggested, but of providing evidence for the differences that exist in schools. For example, if a school claims to be excellent in science and math, then it is reasonable to ask, "How do you know?" If a school claims special success with slow readers, a parent should be able to say, "Show me."

In New York City, the math and reading scores of all 300 elementary schools are published annually. Interestingly, city newspapers do not focus on the highest and the lowest scoring schools or even rank the schools, since such yardsticks fail to account for the disparity among the various districts of the city. Instead, the spotlight is on the schools whose results improve or decline the most over the previous year. These scores are significant as indicators of the life of a school, encouraging a sense of responsibility and accountability between schools and their communities. In some communities in the United States, realtors use average SAT scores of high-performing suburban high schools as one of the selling points for homes in prosperous suburban communities. Such connections, while superficially comforting, may be flawed for the same reason as that revealed by the Ottawa board's research: High test scores match high income areas.

Such readiness to compare school scores stands in marked contrast to the practice in Canada where such comparisons are rarely made. Even within one province (Alberta), city boards disagree on the merits of making comparisons. Edmonton releases the results of provincial diploma exam results by school while Calgary declines to do so. The province of Québec regularly publishes results of provincial exams on a school board by school board basis, without much notable impact on school performance.

Some school-to-school comparisons yield information that educational administrators can use to modify the curriculum and teaching methods. The North York Board of Education's benchmark program, introduced several years ago, focuses on improvements in math and literacy. Using a standard test tied to the North York curriculum, the board analyzes all students in a particular grade, on a rotating basis. Results from testing of Grade 8 math students, for example, show where students are weakest, sparking discussions at the board and school levels on changes in curriculum and teaching methods. Schools with consistently low results are given extra help — more teachers or other special assistance.

Tests developed outside the classroom have the potential to identify weak spots in the curriculum or teaching practices. In North York, for example, the board spent an extra $1.2 million on staff development and curriculum changes between 1990 and 1992 to raise student achievement in mathematics. As a result, student scores on the board's standard test rose by several points over the same period. Any manager in industry understands the importance of quality control data in monitoring and improving the productivity of the system.

North York director of education Veronica Lacey is a strong advocate of testing at the local and national levels. "The whole purpose of testing is to improve performance," she says. But she objects to school-to-school comparisons. "How does it assist (schools) to improve?" she asks. "I haven't seen it work anywhere." One of the myths of testing, Lacey contends, "is that if I publish all the results of how our kids did in the last set of examinations that they would work harder." In practice, only the motivated students are spurred to do better, in her experience. "The good become better and the bad become worse," Lacey argues. "The kids who don't have the self-confidence give up and say, 'Well, I can't compete.'"

For their part, teachers also worry they will be blamed unfairly for poor student results, a fear not without foundation. Early in this century, some jurisdictions practised "payment by results," with teachers compensated in part on the basis of their students' scores on provincial tests. In the early 1980s, as minister of education in British Columbia, William Vander Zalm announced that a proposed new examination system would achieve several objectives, including the "weeding out of bad teachers."

Teachers rightly point out that some students will fail no matter how well they have been taught. Moreover, the face of the classroom has changed dramatically over the past twenty years. The influx of immigrant children who speak neither English nor French as a mother tongue, the integration of children with learning disabilities into the classroom and the social pressures of broken homes and hungry students are significant hurdles for the best of teachers. Nevertheless, some effort should be made to clarify what teachers should be held accountable for and what should be demanded of parents, students and others with a stake in education.

The possible misuse of the results of assessment should not be used as an excuse not to collect data. In jurisdictions where school results are published, there is no apparent evidence of teacher bashing or of weak educational decision making. Indeed, such information can be used to support teachers in the classroom.

The System as a Whole: "How Do We Rate in Comparison with Others?"

What is missing from the Canadian picture is any real mechanism, as yet, to compare student achievement across the country. The first move in this direction is the School Achievement Indicators Program of the Council of Ministers of Education (CMEC), which will test a sample of thirteen- and sixteen-year-olds on their skills in math in 1993 and on reading and writing in 1994. Sensitive to growing public demands for accountability in education, the provincial ministers of education endorsed the project in 1989 as a first-ever national snapshot of a number of education trends, including student performance. The provinces are also being driven to cooperate with each other in the realization that the federal government, with growing interest and investment in education, is an advocate of national testing. While the "national indicators" project marks a first step towards more accountability in education, the results will still be open to interpretation.

As its centrepiece, the $2.5-million CMEC project will make periodic comparisons of "average" student achievement in core areas across the country. In this respect, the project is similar to the cyclical program assessments conducted, increasingly, by all provinces. The national test, based on a representative sample of students from each province, will not allow for school- or board-level comparisons. Nor will the scores be used to assess individual student achievement. Instead, the results will give a broad measure of the overall student success in math, reading and writing, which could lead to changes in curriculum content and teaching methods.

The issue of national testing is a highly charged political issue, as witnessed by the erratic response of Ontario to participation in, first, the CMEC indicators project and, then, the Third International

Mathematics and Science Study that is scheduled to take place in 1994 to 1995. In 1989, under the Liberals, Ontario joined the CMEC project at its inception. Two years later, under the New Democrats, who came to power with strong support from teachers' unions, Ontario pulled out of the project on the grounds that it failed to recognize the social and cultural diversity of students. By late 1991, under a new minister of education, Tony Silipo, Ontario returned to the project with certain key provisos. One key compromise, little publicized at the time, in fact threatens the integrity of the entire program. The memorandum of understanding, negotiated by ministers in December 1991, states that "*at the reporting stage*, any items showing [cultural and gender] bias will be discarded" (emphasis added).[1] Thus if girls do particularly poorly on a specific math item, it could be discarded after the test. Though project officials contend that provinces will be under pressure not to manipulate the test results, the potential for after-the-fact massaging of data is obvious.

The Third International Mathematics and Science Study also represented an about-face for the Ontario Ministry of Education. Having initially agreed to take part in the study, the province withdrew in January 1993, citing the high cost (about $40,000 per year for five years) and a lack of need for the information. After a cabinet shuffle in early February, the new minister, Dave Cooke, reversed course again and pledged Ontario's full participation, recognizing the political imperative to demonstrate accountability. The ambivalence of the educational bureaucrats towards any external assessment of student achievement, however, is almost palpable.

Over the past decade, these international studies have generated a growing level of public attention and controversy; for example, the 1992 International Assessment of Educational Progress gives a picture of what students in a number of countries, including Canada, know about math and science.[2] Not surprisingly, the ranking of countries wins the headlines because it is something that editors — and readers — can get their heads around.

In international comparisons, the tests measure the average performance of a large and (supposedly) representative group of students, in much the same way as an opinion pollster relies on a sample of people to gauge public attitudes. Accordingly, the assumptions that underlie any comparison colour the results. Taken out of context, test scores create a misleading indication of overall educational quality; for example, eighteen-year-old Britons outscore their Canadian counterparts on an international science test. But in the élitist British system, only 10 per cent of eighteen-year-olds, the cream of the crop, take science courses, compared to about 50 per cent of the same age group in Canada. With a larger group representing a wider range of talent and ability, the Canadians would not be expected to do as well as the Britons. Indeed, on closer inspection of the IAEP results, the top-performing Canadian students ranked near the top. These caveats aside, the broad message from these international test results leaves no room for complacency. One troubling conclusion from the IAEP study shows, for example, that Canadian students do reasonably well in their early teens, compared to other students, but lose ground through their mid-teens.

The international studies are an important window on the rest of the world, especially in a country where provincial control has sometimes meant parochial attitudes — "What have I to learn from elsewhere?" They stimulate further inquiry and deeper examination of our own systems in relation to those of others; for example, the Alberta study, which compared curricula and textbooks with those of European and Asian countries, was inspired by the results of international achievement studies.[3]

However difficult to interpret, international comparisons on student achievement are of significant benefit to Canadians. They encourage us to look beyond our own provincial borders to look at how other jurisdictions deal with curriculum and other issues. For example, results from the 1992 International Assessment of Educational Progress show that Canadian students are taught some math and science concepts later than their peers in other countries. The comparison provides fodder for a discussion about possible reforms to write a more challenging curriculum for Canadian students. In the same way, national or interprovincial comparisons can also be useful starting points for discussions about course content and teaching methods. For instance, education researchers are baffled by a pattern that shows student achievement rising from east to west across Canada. No one has an adequate explanation yet, but the issue deserves some careful scrutiny.

In any testing activity, political credibility is crucial: who runs the test and who interprets the results. In British Columbia, for example, the provincial ministry contracts its assessment work to testing experts at local universities. In the United States, the National Assessment of Educational Progress is contracted out to expert assessment teams who are not associated with federal or state departments of education. By contrast, the CMEC School Achievement Indicators project will be conducted by bureaucrats within provincial ministries of education, a "behind-closed-doors" process unlikely to raise public confidence in the results.

Past practices in Ontario illustrate the danger of leaving education insiders in charge of report cards on the system. The provincial ministry conducts annual reviews of student performance similar to assessments conducted in other provinces. Based on a sample of students in certain subjects, the ministry evaluates the system as a whole; for example, a 1992 provincial review examined a sample of math students in Grades 8, 10 and 12. Though the ministry invites some public representation, teachers and ministry officials account for the majority of so-called "interpretation panels," which make subjective assessments of the data collected. The panels rate expected levels of student performance in the subject on a scale from "superior" to "weak" and then compare these expectations to actual results.

Such a subjective interpretation makes it possible to minimize the sting of poor results, if panels have low expectations of how students would perform. Moreover, three of the five labels for student performance — "superior," "strong" and "satisfactory" — carry positive connotations and only the lowest rating — "weak" is negative. In its analysis of Grade 8 math, the panel reported that students were satisfactory to weak in five of six segments of the math curriculum and similarly poor in thirteen of seventeen specific math topics. However, the ministry's rose-coloured conclusion was that "Grade 8 students are achieving at levels judged to be satisfactory or better in more than half of the topics in the mathematics program."[4] An inherent conflict of interest exists when ministries of education are responsible for both the delivery and the assessment of education. The provinces' own curriculum assessment reviews and the CMEC indicators project suffer from the same flaw.

Improving Educational Assessment

One way to raise public confidence in testing would be to set up a Canadian Educational Testing Service (CETS). As a non-governmental organization, the national agency would be comparable to the highly respected, federally funded but politically independent United States Education Testing Service, located on the campus of Princeton University. Operating under the general supervision of our proposed Canadian Education Standards Council and operating at arm's length from both provincial and federal governments, a new Canadian testing agency could serve as an impartial auditor of educational performance across the country.

As a national agency charged with developing and conducting standard tests in a variety of forms, the CETS would work closely with the Canadian Educational Standards Council and with each provincial ministry of education to publish interprovincial comparisons of student achievement in core areas. In addition, it could conduct other types of assessment to provide a more complete picture of educational performance in the country. In this way, Canada could build expertise in educational testing that reflects domestic conditions and needs. A regular program of assessment, conducted by an independent and credible organization, would be a vast improvement over the present patchwork quilt across the country. On its own, a new national assessment program could not raise standards, any more than the X-ray fixes a patient's broken arm. However, a national testing body would provide the information that will help schools and the public set and reach desired educational standards. Moreover, as an apolitical agency, the CETS would do so in a credible and expert manner.

For their own part, the provinces could also undertake two modest reforms: the introduction of minimum competency tests and new mechanisms to raise school accountability. Both reforms are designed to raise educational standards in measurable ways. If students were required to pass minimum competency tests in core subject areas to receive their high school diploma, current rhetorical commitments to "excellence" could be supported and demonstrated with facts.

Such competency tests could be designed to meet the minimum (national) standards expected by the end of high school. In each province, employers, parents and teachers would participate in approving the content of each test, enabling the public to have a larger voice in defining what is expected of schools and students. New York State introduced a minimum competency test several years ago and it now is a standard feature of high school life. Students could take the tests at any time during their high school careers and could retake them as often as needed to pass. This requirement would be in addition to other locally assessed requirements for graduation. The Canadian Education Testing Service could, in time, be the natural agency to assist provinces in developing high-quality tests. Indeed, it would be desirable if, in time, such tests were to become true national competency tests.

The issue of school accountability is an even more politically charged one. Teachers are understandably uneasy about being held to account for the success of all students, when many of the factors affecting their ability and willingness to learn lie well beyond the classroom door. Nevertheless, since teachers count themselves as part of a profession, they should be ready to participate in fair assessments that ensure rewards for effective teaching. At the moment, school boards complain they have little room to weed out incompetent teachers who, at best, are shifted from one school to another if there are enough complaints from students and parents.

For a start, teachers should be required to file complete assessment plans for the courses they teach. School principals should be responsible for the records, which would be reviewed by school boards on a regular basis and available for inspection by the public. In addition, these assessments should be subject to validation by independent testing experts, so as to raise public confidence in the determination of schools to improve quality.

Given the level of public unhappiness over school performance, the testing issue deserves a thorough airing if Canadians are to move from blame to solutions in education. Moreover, education reforms as they relate to testing must strengthen rather than weaken the professional autonomy and effectiveness of teachers. In the case of student assessment, teachers should take more responsibility for communicating with students and parents about what learning occurs in the classroom.

Testing is no panacea for an education system under stress. After all, a mechanic can inspect a car without making the necessary repairs. The route to long-term educational improvement lies with a comprehensive restructuring of the enterprise, not in resorting to the proverbial "quick fix" of a standardized test. The public needs to be informed not only about the growing array of assessment tools, but also about how they should be interpreted to improve student, school and system-wide performance in education. For that reason, testing is only one part of a more comprehensive education restructuring package.

Chapter 7

Sharing
Responsibility

*I*n *London, a* prosperous community in southwestern Ontario where public anger over education has boiled up in recent years, a novel solution to the problem is taking shape. The providers and users of education are working together in an exercise to share responsibility for education.

First, some background. With 46,000 students, the London board is typical of many medium-sized school boards in Ontario in that provincial grants account for a declining share of education revenue. Local property owners, many of them without children in school, have to foot a growing share of the bill — over $160 million of the overall $297.4-million school budget. Like other Ontario communities, London has a grassroots taxpayers' protest group.

Taxpayers are not the only ones voicing concern about education. In 1991, in advance of school board elections, the London Council of Home and School Associations conducted a survey of elementary school parents that showed rising levels of discontent as their children progressed through school. In the survey, 13 per cent of parents with children in the first three grades of school expressed dissatisfaction with schools, but the figure jumped to 23 per cent among parents with children in Grades 7 and 8.

The survey results revealed parental unhappiness on several counts: students' poor spelling, uninformative report cards and an uncommunicative school administration. Among parents of children in Grades 7 and 8 who responded to the survey, more than half complained that the school system was neither accountable to the public nor spent their education dollars well.[1] "Since marks are not given on report cards, it is impossible to know how your child is doing," fumed one parent in comments included in the survey. "The basics are not taught and drilled." Less strident comments from another parent captured the survey's mood of unease about the quality of education in London. "I have very well-behaved children of average intelligence who I feel are being allowed to just slide by," the parent wrote. "They are not being challenged to achieve or motivated to do their best...I am not totally dissatisfied but feel the education system is capable of, and should be, *much more!"* (survey's emphasis).

Even the survey itself proved controversial. Some of the most militant parents, those opposed to the board's introduction of "whole language" reading methods several years earlier, complained that the results were manipulated by the survey's sponsor to soften the negative assessment. Nevertheless, the message seemed to get through to school board trustees and administration officials.

"We hit the wall," says school board chair Cheryl Miller, citing events over the past year, which included an acrimonious meeting between parents and board officials about "whole language" reading methods. Acknowledging the board's failure to communicate well with parents, she says trustees realized they had to rebuild public confidence in the education system or face the consequences. "If we don't make parents out there glad and happy with their kids' education, let me tell you, the provincial government is going to intervene," says Miller, a trustee for the past twelve years.

London's attempt to rebuild confidence recognizes that the public's voice has to be heard more directly in deliberations about the future of education. Like other sectors of the economy, education can no longer afford a top-down approach to decisions that leaves the user of the service out in the cold. With a new director of education appointed in late 1991, the board has turned to critics and supporters to chart a new course for London schools.

Representatives of the home and school organization, parent and taxpayer protest groups, local businesses, teacher unions and school board officials sit on eight task forces in an attempt to hammer out a consensus on goals for education. The "clients" of the system — students, parents, business, special interests and taxpayers — are all voicing significant dissatisfaction with education, says board director Darrel Skidmore. At the same time, he notes, teachers feel undervalued in the face of rising public criticism. The conflict, he argues, shows "there is no consensus around the agenda ....Every one of those groups has their own agenda as to what education should be doing."

Of all the task forces, which include strategic planning and staff development, the one on quality assurance will test whether London will really deliver on its motto "Success for every student." By examining such issues as curriculum, testing and report cards, the quality assurance task force hopes to define clear standards for student performance that will, in turn, make the system more accountable to parents and the public.

The exercise in London is worth some scrutiny because it raises high expectations about reforms that promise to share power and responsibility for education in new ways. On the surface, the education establishment seems to be willing to relinquish some of its control over the agenda. But is the London exercise in consensus building serious? Cynics could interpret the effort as political window dressing. The task forces, for example, remain firmly in the hands of the education "insiders," including board administrators, who account for two-thirds of the membership. Those of a more optimistic bent will interpret the London experiment as long overdue recognition that the ground rules for education have changed. With task force discussions only in their early phase in 1993, the jury is still out. However, the risks for the London board are high, since failure would heighten cynicism about public education.

One of the toughest critics of the process is parent Bonnie Cumming, a member of the quality assurance task force. The mother of three children in elementary and secondary schools, she felt deeply unhappy over what she saw as mediocre school standards and organized a fledgling parent protest group in 1992. As the task force began its deliberations in the fall of 1992, Cumming says she was "cautiously optimistic" that the exercise would yield results. "I feel that Mr. Skidmore genuinely wants to develop a better partnership." But from personal experience she is disillusioned with teachers and school officials who talk the language of change without implementing it. "We have always been heard, I think, but not 'actioned' upon," says Cumming, who wants schools to provide more structure, content and rigour for students. "It's different [for the schools] to listen and to actually do something with what [they] are hearing." Two months into the process, she sounds less optimistic that her specific concerns will be addressed. "I'm the mouse at the base of the mountain," she says, acknowledging she is outnumbered on the task force.

Bonnie Cumming's experiences give her grounds for scepticism about whether the education establishment is serious about closing the gap between the rhetoric and reality of reform. Like many parents, she hears the promises of "quality assurance" and "essential learnings" but sees a different story in the classroom. Alarmed when her middle child, Greg, encountered difficulty in spelling, reading and grammar, she has lobbied teachers, board officials and trustees without receiving adequate answers. She has become a pointed critic of "whole language" reading methods because Greg, now in Grade 6, still struggles to spell words such as with ("whith"), desire ("decier") and therefore ("thairfor"). His Grade 6 teacher rates him at a Grade 3 spelling level. Despite Cumming's stated concerns at the time, Greg's Grade 4 report card offered no clue about his weak spelling. "He has displayed good interest in the spelling program," the teacher reported in her year-end evaluation. "The quality of his written work has improved."

Cumming says she and her husband would enrol their children in private school if they had the means. Unable to pursue that option, this working mother has opted to invest time and energy in the task force exercise in hopes that her concerns will be addressed in time. She wants teachers made more accountable for results, so that problems like those experienced by her son do not fester beneath the surface of a "don't worry, be happy" school philosophy. Though the London board conducts city-wide tests of students in Grades 3, 6 and 9, Cumming complains that the results are not shared with parents on a systematic basis. "I don't see why the results cannot automatically be mailed to the parents."

School board chair Miller says trustees cannot afford to ignore public concerns about education. "We have entered this long path because it eventually leads to more accountability," says Miller. "To make education more of a shared responsibility, it has to be a system instead of the 'royal order' from the top." Even so, she sees political risks for trustees. "The board has brought in this whole process [the task forces] knowing full well that when the reports come in, we are going to have to do something about them. If we shelve them, we are going to have our ass in a swing because we have got too many people from the community who have become involved. So we have committed ourselves. It's kind of a scary thing, because I don't know what the outcome is."

Others on the quality assurance task force also recognize that inaction on the part of those traditionally influential in the education agenda carries a high price. As president of the Ontario Secondary School Teachers' Federation in London, Bill Brooks says organizations such as his must shoulder some of the blame for the public's jaded view of teachers. "We have earned partly the reputation that we have achieved. That's what the federation has to turn around," says Brooks. As a member of the quality assurance task force, Brooks hopes the discussions will provide an opportunity for teachers to work co-operatively with school officials and the public. "I would like to see a new commitment on the part of the partners to find out what each other feels about education."

In the end, he says, quality assurance means providing parents with "good, first-rate knowledge" about what is happening at school. But he says parents are not alone in their unease about new trends that are cloaked in the jargon of education. "Parents aren't the only ones who say, 'I don't understand half the language that's being used in education today.' Teachers don't understand all that either."

As a business representative on the task force, consulting engineer Peter van der Westen applauds the London exercise as a vital step towards needed reforms. "We do have all the stakeholders at the table. So if it fails, we are all going to be blamed — business, educators, parents. If this is window dressing, then it's our own fault. All the tools are in place, so it's up to us."

With school reform getting top political billing in all provinces, there is growing acceptance that education cannot be left to the experts. But Cumming and other members of the public are right to be dubious about the willingness of the traditional players — ministry bureaucracies and teachers' unions — to share power and demonstrate greater public accountability. However, the mark of a reinvented system is its recognition that traditional roles and responsibilities must be redefined so that those who use the education system are not shut out of decisions.

Unfortunately, the rhetoric of education today is long on words such as *partnership, collaboration* and *empowerment* and short on measurable results. In fact, the words of change most readily slip off the tongues of those seen as opposed to change. "Education is not the exclusive domain of educators," observes the Ontario Teachers' Federation in a 1992 submission to the Ontario cabinet, which called for genuine collaboration in education.[2] These days, every ministry of education and school board trumpets "partnerships," especially with business, to show their commitment to better relations with the world beyond the schoolyard. However, the political reality of education in the 1990s is that there is a serious breakdown in trust between those who provide the education service and those who use it.

A recent school meeting in Milton, Ontario, drives home the point. As the principals from two local high schools tried to explain Ontario curriculum changes proposed for Grade 9 students in September 1993, the parents listened with polite but visible scepticism. The most controversial proposal — to eliminate the practice of grouping of students in Grade 9 by perceived level of ability — drew the most pointed questions. But the parents were also worried about plans to eliminate Grade 9 subject credits so that students would move on to Grade 10 regardless of their performance.

As the questions grew more sceptical in tone, the school principals found themselves in an increasingly awkward position. At first,
they tried to sell the curriculum changes as essential for students to
become flexible, creative thinkers. But as time went on, under sus-
tained grilling, one of the principals acknowledged that the proposals
were "ministry mandates" en route to implementation.

In effect, despite the appearance of consultation and involvement, the Milton parents and their children had no way to influence
the course of events. "I'm not sure anything's improving," groused
one parent. The gulf between the promise of co-operation and the
practice of one-way communications by education bureaucrats, by
no means unique to Ontario, explains why the Canadian public is
increasingly jaded about education. "Collaboration seems to be
gaining an important foothold in a system that is not designed to be
really collaborative," observes the Ontario Teachers' Federation in
its document to the Ontario cabinet.[3]

The current system does not acknowledge the right of the users
of the education system to have an influential voice in determining
how to improve school quality. To be sure, every conceivable interest group is represented on advisory bodies to provincial governments. Ontario, for example, has a learners' advisory council with
no fewer than fifty-two representatives from a cross-section of education interest groups, but the sheer size and diversity of such a
group guarantees no clear decisions. In any case, since ministry
bureaucrats, teachers and school boards have a majority voice on
the council, the educational establishment remains in complete
control of the policy agenda.

However, the walls are beginning to close in on these élites.
Taxpayer fury in Scarborough, Ontario, over school board trustees
who voted themselves a huge pay raise in the middle of the recession now has the Ontario premier musing aloud about disman-

tling school boards. Parents' groups such as those in London and other communities are becoming more vocal. The business community has started to pay attention to issues of education quality almost on a par with tax and trade policy. If education is to become truly a shared responsibility, then we should ask who the stakeholders are and what their roles should be in a reinvented education system.

Who Are the Partners in Education?

The dissonant voices now heard in education show how the traditional lines of authority have broken down. Parents, students, employers and other consumers of education now demand a larger say in what goes on at school. Though their interests and agendas are by no means compatible, they send the same message that business-as-usual practices are no longer acceptable. "The common theme," observes Veronica Lacey, director of the North York Board of Education, is that all "feel that they are not enough involved in the decisions."

Some of the traditional players in education are also looking for other ways to influence the process. Universities and community colleges, for example, are forging stronger connections with elementary and secondary schools to improve the quality of graduates. Students who arrive at post-secondary institutions lacking essential skills in reading, math and science become expensive liabilities likely to drop out before graduation. As it is, universities and colleges now offer remedial programs for freshmen and other undergraduates who lack the most basic writing and math skills.

Let us consider some of the schools' partners in the education process: students, parents and members of the community — from business, universities and colleges, and community services.

Listen to the Learners

On a chilly winter's night in Toronto, Grade 12 students Elisha Yoder and Lisa Bzdurreck are working hard on school business. As two of three elected student representatives on the school management council at Rosedale Heights Secondary School, they are symbols of democracy in action. The council is one of several innovations in the delivery of education programs and services at the inner-city school in Toronto. Composed of equal numbers of parents, students and teachers, the council advises the principal on policy issues affecting the school. With more authority than a traditional home and school organization, the two-year-old council was instrumental in developing a new report card. But, unlike some elected councils in the United States, the Rosedale Heights group does not control the budget or hire staff.

For the two students, the council meeting provides an unparalleled opportunity to lobby for long-promised improvements in the library. "Every other school has a library," complains Elisha, citing a severe shortage of reference works in a library originally intended to serve a younger group of non-academic students. "As a student, [I find it] almost insulting," Elisha tells the council. "Adults don't know what's going on at the library," adds Lisa. Principal Barry Sketchley, a non-voting member of the council, backs up Elisha's assessment. In response, the council decides to redouble its efforts to prise the funds from the Toronto board, which had promised to fund library improvements several years ago as part of a comprehensive effort to revitalize the school.

Though most affected by decisions about school, students rarely have a voice in the process. However, as the Rosedale Heights example makes clear, students have much to contribute to make the school more relevant for all. Students also need to take more responsibility for their academic lives. In British Columbia, students early in high school are expected to draft a "personalized learning plan" as a means to help them make better-informed choices about study programs and career options. In the final two years of high school, career planning is one of four components of the academic program in British Columbia. Students are required to meet regularly with teachers and mentors for counselling.

For students, North American society sends mixed signals about the value of education. A different message is delivered in Asian countries. Researchers observe that in Japan and China, for instance, students are encouraged to work hard to achieve their academic goals.[4] In these cultures, effort is one of the factors seen as explaining differences in achievement, with some students willing to put in extra time and hard work to learn what is expected of them. High expectations, however, are not embedded in education practices and beliefs in North America. In the jargon of education, students are given "opportunities to learn," as if discipline and hard work were not essential to success at school. In contrast to Asian cultures, North American society is more likely to explain differences in achievement on the basis of innate ability. As a result, some students are seen as less able than others to master certain concepts.

Accordingly, North Americans are less inclined to brand students as failures if they are not academically successful. The parallel is also true: As a society we do little to encourage students to aim high in school. For young people, heroes are defined in narrow terms as those who demonstrate athletic prowess or success in show business. Indeed, the definition may include those who might have left school at Grade 10 and gone on to make a fortune. As a society, we pay a price for setting low expectations in education. If we want our children to become their best in their chosen field of endeavour, we must confront the mixed messages delivered at home, at school and by society in general.

One of the negative consequences of putting so much stress on ability as a determinant of academic success is that schools stream some students into less challenging academic programs. Typically, the losers are poor and minority students who, in being shuffled into less demanding programs, are deprived of a quality educational experience. The practice simply exacerbates existing social tensions. At last, many educational professionals now recognize that all children, regardless of their perceived ability, need learning environments that stimulate and challenge them.

Setting high expectations is a new theme in Canadian education reform. The strongest message from the 1992 New Brunswick inquiry on education was the need for schools and families to raise their sights for student success. "Perhaps the greatest obstacle to excellence in our schools is not a lack of resources, human or material; nor is it the organizational structure — though all these could be improved. It is rather the lack of high expectations and their more tangible expression, high standards," the inquiry concluded.[5]

Still, the mixed messages continue. British Columbia and Alberta have beefed up their high school graduation awards for top students, but Ontario eliminated its scholarships for top-level high-school graduates as a cost-saving measure in 1991. If students are to take responsibility for learning, they will need to be shown by word and deed the value of hard work. As the Confucian philosopher Hsun Tzu observed:

> Achievement consists of never giving up....If there is no dark and dogged will, there will be no shining accomplishment; if there is no dull and determined effort, there will be no brilliant achievement.[6]

All students can learn. All have the right to the most effective environment possible for learning. Equally, we must recognize that some will need to work harder than others to reach their goals. But lectures on the value of hard work will be lost on the wind unless adults serve as credible role models. In urging students to aim high, teachers and parents will also need to explain why students should work hard — and to what ends.

In others words, demanding that students take more responsibility for learning means that they should be heard on issues that affect their performance at school. In some schools, for example, students set goals for themselves and assess their progress, starting in Grade 3. Other schools turn to mentoring, improved guidance services, co-operative education and other partnerships to send the message about hard work and high expectations. Expect a lot; get a lot. The best teachers can create a desire to learn where none exists; in the end, though, students must do the work.

Parents as Partners

Researchers have long recognized the crucial role of the family in fostering educational success. Citing research on parental involvement at all stages of a student's school career, a 1987 research paper by the Toronto Board of Education observed that "the influence of the home on children's success is profound."[7] Yet reforms that recognize the powerful role of parents as partners have been slow to materialize. For better or worse, parents make an enormous difference through the values they instill and the sacrifices they make. "Education is a three-way partnership between student, parent and teacher," says Alan Herbert, a parent and chairman of the Rosedale Heights management council. "The outcome is totally dependent on all three partners. Parents who abdicate their responsibility have as much influence as the parent who does participate."

In many homes across Canada, parents put a premium on learning, whether through reading to their children from the earliest age, assistance with homework or support for extra-curricular activities. Parents today are more vigilant and demanding than in the past, says school principal Margery Higginson, of Delta, British Columbia. "Parents are much less willing to say okay, you are going to school, I'll trust your teacher is doing a good job."

Regrettably, in other families, students receive little encouragement, and success may come in spite of an unsupportive environment. Fredericton teacher Ed Bujold recalls the response of one parent to complaints about her child's absence from school. The parent claimed the student was at home, though Bujold could see him smoking with friends just off school property. "We've got to get back to societal values," says Bujold, who urges parents to play their part in demanding excellence from students. "We have to have a heck of a lot more than lip service for [excellence] from the home."

Parental attitudes to education also vary among cultures. In his study of Japanese family values, Merry White, author of *The Japanese Educational Challenge*, describes the influential role of Japanese mothers in setting high expectations for their children at an early age.[8] But comparisons between Japanese and North American societies are fraught with difficulty because U.S. and Canadian women, unlike their Asian counterparts, are significant participants in the workforce. Other yardsticks show how family values vary among societies. U.S. researchers Harold Stevenson and James Stigler note that 98 per cent of Japanese and 95 per cent of Chinese families provide a study area and desk at home, compared to 63 per cent of American families.[9] By setting aside a quiet area for students to work, parents send a strong message about the importance of learning.

The message must also be reinforced by schools themselves. From the opening day of school in September, students at Elia Middle School in North York, Ontario, are assigned homework. "We establish from day one that we want to see every child going home with books. I want it to be a pattern," says principal Hugh Beattie. "What we are building is the idea that while school occurs here, learning also continues at home." At Elia, an inner-city school with more than forty different languages spoken, homework is assigned on a regular basis, with daily logs showing parents what is expected of their children. The school coaches parents on how to be home tutors and suggests ways to foster a supportive learning environment at home. For their part, parents are expected to monitor the student's work to see that it is completed — and done well.

The message on homework, part of a North York board policy, shows how schools can build bridges to the community instead of walls. Several years ago, the board surveyed parents and found a deep concern over the erratic commitment of schools to homework assignments — for parents, a symbol of academic beliefs and values. North York now requires all schools to include homework in their school improvement plans, which are developed in consultation with parents, teachers and students.

Parents play the primary role in supporting their own children's learning. With more local autonomy, parents would also be among those expected to shape the educational life of their community. As participants in community school councils, they would play a more direct part than is now possible in defining the goals and values of their school — in conjunction with others in the community. In some communities, this is beginning to happen. In others, it could happen once legislative authority was transferred from the school boards. Other communities may not be ready to take on the responsibility of operating their own school; in all cases, significant community and parent training will be needed before such a transfer of power can take place. The lesson from experiences elsewhere with local decision making is that the process is labour-intensive and time-consuming. Parents and other community representatives will need a reservoir of patience, wisdom and commitment to build schools with character.

Even without a formal transfer of power to the local level, schools can take steps to reach out to parents. Steve Lawton, professor of education at the Ontario Institute for Studies in Education, says information is the key to accountability at all levels of education: "I don't feel there's a lot of communication between the school and the parent." He suggests that each school publish a budget that shows what it costs to educate children and a report card on school attendance and other factors that give a portrait of student life. Such information might well help the school, parents and others in the community find ways to improve achievement and counter dropouts. Without communication, members of the community cannot be expected to know how they can help at school.

Each school has a personality shaped by history, people and circumstance, as Ottawa parent Heather Smith can attest. A mother of two elementary school children and active in education reform issues in her community, Smith and her husband were about to send their first child to kindergarten six years ago. The local school sent out pages of rules and regulations for students and parents. Unhappy with an approach that emphasized form over content, the Smiths explored other options in the area and chose Churchill Alternative School, a public school created in 1984 in response to active parents.

Owing to its history as a parent-inspired alternative school, Churchill has a four-page statement of philosophy, based on the active involvement of students, parents and staff in the life of the school. The school recognizes parents as partners in the education of their children and gives them opportunities to participate in planning, organizing and implementing programs for students, parents and staff.

Smith is enthusiastic about the school because "there's a sense of shared goals and achievements," with teachers, parents and students seen as members of the same team. Churchill believes in child-centred learning, hands-on activities, multi-age groupings of students who stay with the same teacher for several years — practices that flow from the education philosophy of the Swiss educator and thinker Jean Piaget. As well, parents are actively involved in the day-to-day life of the school. "There's a relationship of trust and respect," says Smith, praising the school's open-door policy.

But not all schools in the Ottawa board have the same parent-oriented philosophy as Churchill. When the Smiths moved their eleven-year old daughter, Elizabeth, to a nearby elementary school with a gifted program not available at Churchill, they found a less friendly environment. "I don't feel as welcome in my daughter's class," says Smith, citing the need to schedule visits at the larger school. At the 400-student alternative school, she is warmly greeted when she drops into her son Derek's Grade 4 class unannounced.

Churchill Alternative principal Donna Belanger says, "Communication is of the utmost importance." In her view, teachers, parents and students form three overlapping circles, each group with individual and collective responsibilities. From Grade 2, students are taught to set goals for themselves and evaluate their own progress through the school. Parents help set expectations for their children in consultation with teachers at the beginning of the year.

Parents do not have all the answers, but they cannot abandon education issues to the bureaucracy either. The road to educational excellence cannot be travelled by schools alone. The issue of homework is a case in point. Parents complain that teachers are erratic about giving students extra written work after school. But teachers see little point in assigning homework when parents allow their children to work after-hours instead of hitting the books on week nights. Parents must shoulder their part of the load to support schools in setting standards and imparting values.

Building Bridges to the Community

Schools are a physical presence in every community. In striking a new deal with the public, schools must find a way to close the "intellectual" distance from those beyond the school gate. Too often, schools shroud themselves in a cloud of abstraction, making it impossible to carry on a useful conversation with the outside world. For a growing segment of the public, those with no children in school, the only involvement in education occurs when they pay local property taxes. Schools need to open new lines of communication with the community to discuss ways they can support each other in the learning enterprise. In September 1992, the Corporate-Higher Education Forum, a national group of business and university leaders based in Montréal, published six goals for education, including that "each community work together to create and sustain an appropriate effective school environment focused on achievement."[10] As it is, many schools are already used in off-hours for adult education and community functions. But schools have some distance to go if their goal is to become flexible, multi-use institutions geared to the needs of youth throughout the day. A first step would be for the community to establish political control of its schools. In addition, closer relations must develop between the school and all segments of the community: business, higher education and community social services.

Partnerships with Business

Links between schools and the business community have been growing for the past decade in Canada, echoing trends in the United States. As an increasingly vocal critic of education, business demands a bigger say in school performance. It is one thing to be able to influence national standards or the direction of provincial policy. Such a form of involvement is ideal from the business perspective: maximum impact for minimum effort. A true partnership with schools, however, demands a much higher degree of commitment and involvement at the community level — for members of the business community as much as for parents.

In the United States, the National Center for Educational Statistics reports a rapid growth in school-business partnerships from 42,200 to 140,800 in the four-year period ending in 1987, 12 per cent of which were targeted at math and science projects.[11] While the number of school-business partnerships in Canada is on the rise, no formal statistics on the topic have been kept. The Conference Board of Canada, which has organized three national conferences on business-education partnerships, has not compiled a comprehensive list to document the growth in recent years. However, the board has established national awards for innovative partnerships and has published a report on the ingredients required for a successful partnership.[12]

With the United States having a longer track record in school-business partnerships than Canada, more research has emerged in that country on their effectiveness. The New York-based Carnegie Corporation, a supporter of many types of education alliances, reviewed what had been learned in science-related projects in the five years up to 1988.[13] Successful partnerships, not surprisingly, benefited from strong leaders in the school and from corporations who understood the projects' purposes. The best projects started small, establishing a niche for the activity before getting bigger. While the successful projects had adequate funds for the start-up and follow-through, they prospered because of the strong participation of volunteers, such as scientists, in the classroom.

Some of the most exciting school-business partnerships in Canada are found in the form of co-operative education programs. The Co-operative, Career and Work Education Association of Canada, a national organization of government, business, education and community groups, estimates that the number of secondary school students enrolled in co-op education programs has more than doubled since 1987, to a total of 140,000 in 1992.[14] The organization says that co-op education is the fastest growing program in Canadian high schools. Although originally designed for vocational students and students in academic difficulty, co-op education is now seen as a tool for all students to explore potential careers.

School-business partnerships are not without risk. For companies that "adopt a school" and do little else, the supposed partnership is little more than a public relations gesture. A second risk is that business will tire of its new-found interest in education. Working with students is a labour-intensive activity that demands commitment from the classroom to the community at large. As U.S. researchers Marsha Levine and Roberta Trachtman discovered, the companies that had the most successful partnerships with schools were those that had the patience to take the long-term view: "Effective partnerships take time."[15]

Partnerships with Universities and Colleges

Post-secondary institutions have a vested interest in reaching out to elementary and secondary schools. In all provinces, government grants to post-secondary education are shrinking in real terms so that universities and community colleges can ill afford the high turnover of students who fail to make the grade after first year. At the same time, universities are under pressure to reach out to poor and minority students who are under-represented in current enrolment figures. Moreover, with almost all provinces engaged in reviews of post-secondary education, universities and colleges are being forced to demonstrate their value to the community as never before.

For all these reasons, the post-secondary sector is looking to play a larger role in the life of high school students. Concern over the number of girls who drop science and math in high school, for example, has spawned a number of joint projects between universities and high schools. One project is a summer research program at the University of Alberta sponsored by Women in Scholarship, Engineering, Science and Technology (WISEST) for girls entering Grade 12. Under the direction of Margaret Ann Armour of the University of Alberta chemistry department, more than forty girls are selected as summer interns for research teams in the university's science and engineering faculties (also, boys, in smaller numbers, are selected for internships in the university's nursing and home economics faculties). After eight years of operation, WISEST reports that 80 per cent of the interns go on to study in the fields in which they worked in the summer. The students credit the WISEST program for being influential in their career decisions. Inspired by the success of the Alberta program, York University, located in one of the most ethnically diverse neighbourhoods in the country, has launched a similar program to attract minority students to science and environmental studies.

Partnerships with Community Social Services

The changing structure of the family — and the economy — in Canada makes it difficult for some Canadian families to fulfil their obligations to their children. Many single-parent families are led by women with incomes below the poverty line. Increasingly, teachers say they cannot do their best for children who come to school without adequate sleep or food. In every province, large school boards now budget for hot breakfast and lunch programs so that students are physically ready to learn. Both government and business have a role to play in encouraging family participation in schools, through improved child-care services. As a study by Statistics Canada reports, "If the present trends in family structure and female labour force participation continue, Canada is likely to face an increased demand for extra-familial care — in spite of a low fertility rate."[16] Once again, although Ottawa and business groups are quick to criticize education quality, they are slow to fulfil their obligations on supportive policies for adequate, affordable child-care facilities.

In Kentucky, where parental involvement is a cornerstone of state-wide education reforms, a citizen's watch-dog group on education cites several key ingredients needed to make parents full partners in school success. The list from the Prichard Committee for Academic Excellence in Kentucky, which has lobbied for education reforms for the past decade, includes "family friendly" policies at work and school, parent co-operation in setting high expectations for students and the removal of barriers between families and schools. "Successful school reform requires fundamental changes that go beyond the schools themselves," comments Robert Sexton, executive director of the Prichard Committee. "To reform schools we have to do more than *just* reform schools. We have to address the way communities raise their children."[17] One way in which Kentucky is providing for that is by establishing Family Resource Centers and Youth Services Centers "to help students and their families with problems which interfere with learning such as poverty, family difficulties, and substance abuse."[18] These centres are being established in or near schools to make them more available to both schoolchildren and members of their families.

In Canada, the funding crunch is forcing health, welfare and other public services, including education, to collaborate on the provision of youth services. The Ontario Premier's Council on Health, Well-Being and Social Justice has been studying pilot projects that would integrate youth services at the school level. In New Brunswick, the provincial government has added funds for preventive early childhood education as part of its overall education reforms. In British Columbia, education and social services agencies work jointly to help pregnant teens and teenage mothers stay in school.

These trends drive home the point that education is a collective responsibility of the community. One cannot promise educational excellence without clearing the path for its achievement at school. Every effort must be made to ensure that all children, from the earliest age, do not lose ground unnecessarily. Otherwise, a higher price will be paid later in school drop-outs, alienated youth and expensive support systems for those who have lost their way. Tight budgets in all provinces have the potential to spark innovations in the delivery of youth services in the community.

Conclusion

In a recent book on how to improve the public schools in the United States, American journalist Larry Martz writes:

> There's good news in this book: We can make our schools better for our kids. We don't have to wait for [the government] to act. We don't have to stand by while "experts" in ivory towers squabble over cures for the epidemic of mediocrity that is sapping our children's minds and threatening our country's future. We can simply take action to make the schools better for teaching kids. Not perfect, but better. Maybe a lot better.[19]

Ours is a good news message, too. Canadians have it within their power to improve their schools. But to transform that power into action requires the development of a new mindset. Education cannot be left to the experts; equally, the solutions do not lie in blind criticisms of those who now manage the system. As individuals, and as members of interest groups, Canadians must demand more of themselves in order to take responsibility for their schools.

Taking responsibility means more than making decisions at the local level to hire and fire, to apportion the budget and to adopt a new curriculum. Canadians must commit their time and creativity to supporting the work of learning both in the home and through their businesses, through their community social agencies, through the churches, associations and clubs, through their institutions of higher education and in every other way imaginable. In taking that degree of responsibility, we shall be working with the schools to reinvent education for our children.

Chapter 8

Learning from Experience

*T*he *real paradox* of teachers, schools and the overall education system is that while they believe themselves to be in the "learning business," they are themselves among the slowest of learners. One teacher's special expertise in a specific area of the curriculum, such as mathematics, does not readily get shared among other teachers in the same school. One school's innovative approach to communicating with parents only rarely spreads to others in the same school board. The work done in one board on developing program materials for elementary science, for example, is painstakingly redone in the adjacent one. And despite the existence of the Council of Ministers of Education, few innovations in one province influence directions taken in the next. In education, it appears, we are condemned forever to "reinventing the wheel."

Peter Senge, author of a recent book on the changing corporate culture, predicts that companies and institutions that put a premium on learning have the best chance to survive and prosper in the future. He writes, "Learning disabilities are tragic in children, especially where they go undetected. They are no less tragic in organizations, where they also go largely undetected."[1] The public education system is desperately in need of reform and improvement, but another set of policy changes imposed on schools from outside will not transform the basic mindset. Education needs to drop the static, passive attitude of waiting to receive orders in favour of a dynamic entrepreneurial outlook, where old problems are transformed into new opportunities for growth. To use Senge's metaphor, it is not enough to teach educators new lessons if the underlying disability is not to be corrected.

Bringing about such a change of culture is easier said than done. As the British comedy series "Yes Minister" reminds us, self-preservation is the *raison d'être* of any bureaucracy. In this respect, the education system is no different, especially now when teachers and schools are under attack. However, schools will not flourish if teachers and others in the system hunker down in hopes of waiting out the storm. Instead, teachers and their critics must explore new approaches that will help the system and those who work in it must develop a strong capacity for self-renewal.

Although the hierarchical nature of the education system in Canada can be held responsible for many of its outdated and ineffective practices, school cannot be reformed through structural alterations alone. New structures must be matched with new attitudes, as Canadian business is also discovering as it seeks to become more competitive. New attitudes must be developed at every level of the system, from ministries of education, through school administrators and classroom teachers to parents and members of the public. In reinventing Canadian education, we need to ensure that the education system is sensitive to the changes in the world outside the school and innovative in its response. In the words of the title of a new project of the Ontario Teachers' Federation, we must focus on "creating a culture of change,"[2] and the place to start must be with teachers themselves.

Three issues must be addressed if the education system is to transform itself into a true learning organization: the professional status and education of teachers, attitudes towards innovation in schools, and the role of research and development in education. The teaching profession and the public are equally ambiguous about the training, certification and career development required for those involved in the school enterprise. Central to this ambiguity is a general lack of consensus over the responsibilities of teachers with respect to innovation in teaching and the role of school principals in encouraging innovation and change. Finally, and of no less importance, the absence of a strong Canadian tradition of education research and development means that those inside and outside the classroom fail to learn from their own and others' experience.

In recent years, there has been no shortage of voices calling for action to improve teaching and research in Canada. Provincial government inquiries, as well as university, business and teacher groups, have all sounded appeals for reforms aimed at raising the professional status of teachers and building a stronger foundation of research and innovation in education.[3] Despite these warnings over the past two years, the education system shows only a few signs of addressing issues of teacher development, innovation or research and development. Together, these hold the keys to the ongoing renewal of public education in Canada. Taking responsibility for Canada's schools must not be a case simply of a change of ownership. It must also represent a change of culture: from one of passive obedience (or secret resistance) to outside directives to one of active innovation in the face of continuous change.

Professionalism in Teaching

Teachers are the lightning rods of the school system. They are the first point of contact for students and parents, a lasting reminder of one's own educational experience[4] and a direct target for public unease about slipping school standards. Sit down with disaffected parents, employers and taxpayers these days and the air flashes with complaints. Bluntly stated, critics see teachers as unionized fat cats who enjoy relatively high pay and job security, long summer holidays and frequent professional days, but who show little regard for results.

Indeed, teachers are better educated and better paid and have better pensions and benefits than fifty years ago. However, sit down with teachers across the country, and they quickly identify the factors that make their job so difficult: hungry and troubled students, shrinking education dollars, uninvolved parents and top-down directives. "We live in a 'them and us' situation," laments one teacher. In addition, many classroom teachers are jaded by the promise of change that never seems to produce lasting improvement. Academic credits are in, then they are out; semestering is in, then it is abandoned. The disillusionment comes through strongly in a national survey of the profession by Queen's University for the Canadian Teachers' Federation in 1992. One Grade 3 teacher in New Brunswick objected to the band-wagon approach to change in education. "A parade of new ideas has come through our district. Great amounts of time and money have been spent on these ideas only to see them replaced by the next new idea." The Queen's study, the most comprehensive national survey of teacher attitudes ever conducted, showed that 18 per cent of those surveyed would not choose teaching again, despite the salary and prestige. Another 10 per cent say the job is not what they expected and would leave within three years of qualifying. Another 9 per cent said they were actively seeking another career.[5]

Despite these feelings, many more young people are seeking entry to the teaching profession than there are places for them; faculties of education turn away eight or nine applicants for every one accepted. Yet the profession and the public harbour uncertainty about the education and training needed to make a good teacher.[6] Similarly, since teaching demands more of its practitioners over time, there is also uncertainty about the kind of ongoing education and career development teachers need to carry out their responsibilities with distinction.

Given their diverse responsibilities for the intellectual and emotional life of students, teachers themselves receive only a modest amount of education and training. The academic requirements have risen, of course, since the 1960s, with the transfer of teachers' colleges (formerly normal schools) to university faculties of education. Until then, teachers needed only a high school diploma and a stint at ministry-run colleges before arriving for their duties in the classroom. All provinces now expect teachers to have a larger world view, requiring an undergraduate degree together with a teaching qualification. In some universities, a Bachelor of Education degree is granted on the basis of a first degree with an additional year (an eight-month academic year) of teacher education at the faculty of education. In others, prospective teachers combine their undergraduate and teacher education studies over the same five-year period. In some cases, a student can take education as a field of undergraduate studies over a four-year period, but receive only a B.Ed.

Teacher education is designed as a two-part activity, with some theoretical preparation in the university classroom followed by hands-on practical experience in the field. However, the time allotted for both theory and practice is so short that many now question the effectiveness of teacher education programs. In some one-year programs, for example, student teachers spend only twenty weeks learning about theories of education and teaching strategies. For the balance of the program in some jurisdictions, student teachers spend as little as ten weeks in elementary and secondary classrooms observing the experienced professionals and developing their own teaching skills. The "on-the-job" practice is a key part of the process, a high-stakes experience that will determine whether the student teacher is recommended for certification.

Put simply, a one-year program (or its equivalent, spread out over several years) does not give prospective teachers long enough to acquire the intellectual grounding, the technical skills and the personal development for success in today's schools. But provincial ministries of education so far are not prepared to pay for more. In some areas of the curriculum, such as math and science, incoming elementary school teachers need significantly more time at university to gain enough confidence to teach these subjects effectively. And at all school levels in urban areas, teachers need much more time to study the complex social contexts in which they will be working when they graduate.

Once teachers receive their initial certification, they are not required to take more training. In practice, many teachers do take additional courses to diversify their qualifications. The brief duration of teacher education, coupled with the light intellectual load of the programs themselves, tends to reinforce a negative public view of the profession. The perception is that teacher education lacks substance and intellectual rigour and that being a teacher is essentially an easy task not worthy of added educational preparation or professional status.

Despite the rhetoric of lifelong learning, Canadian teachers have few incentives to pursue graduate studies in education or to enrol in other forms of training and career development. What salary-related incentives exist are still geared to the days when teachers often lacked even a bachelor's degree. These incentives need to be reviewed and, in many cases, the standards substantially upgraded. In the United States, some states are establishing higher standards for the teaching profession; for example, New York State now will grant a permanent teaching certificate only after completion of a Master's degree and a period of successful teaching. In other jurisdictions, teachers are required to renew their certificate at regular intervals, showing evidence of professional growth, or it will expire.

There are some promising signs that Canadian universities are giving new thought to the difficult task of teacher education; for example, several universities are now designing new programs that effectively lengthen the period of teacher preparation from one to two years. The University of Western Ontario now proposes to scrap its B.Ed. program in favour of a two-year Master's degree program to allow for more rigorous intellectual development and hands-on experience. One important benefit of an extended program is that student teachers would have more time to integrate what they learn about the theory of education with what they experience in the school classroom. "We must create new courses, new structures and new ways of delivering our services," argue the authors of the UWO proposal. "What we are creating is not another undergraduate program but a graduate program of professional education."[7]

The direction in teacher education now being taken by the University of Western Ontario and other universities is promising. However, as a society, Canadians must recognize that we have set, and will continue to set, higher expectations of teachers year by year. Accordingly, we must do more than simply upgrade the current system of training them. Instead, we must re-examine the current structure of the teaching profession and traditional approaches to the education and training of teachers, with a view to enhancing the status of teachers as professionals. If teachers are treated more like professionals, then we can expect they will behave more like professionals. If they are treated like bureaucrats, they will act like bureaucrats. With this in mind, we have three suggestions: transferring control of the teaching profession from governments to the profession itself; raising the standards for entry to and promotion within teaching; and broadening the range of educational opportunities.

A College of Teachers

Teachers in our society are nominally professionals but lack features that characterize other professionals, such as accountants, doctors and lawyers: self-regulation, the setting of training standards and rigorous academic preparation. Given the high expectations for teachers, some structural reforms are needed to foster a higher degree of professional autonomy — and accountability.

One such route would be the establishment of a Canadian College of Teachers, which would act as the gatekeeper for admission to the profession in place of provincial ministries of education. Such a body would ideally be national in scope if the provinces and the teachers' organizations chose to co-operate in creating a single entity. However, given the limited enthusiasm for interprovincial projects in education, a more likely scenario would be the establishment of twelve separate colleges. In any event, these new bodies would be made up of teachers and representatives of the public who would define standards for entry, maintenance of professional standing, teacher education and certification. As in medicine and law, a college of teachers would be responsible for setting and policing ethical standards of conduct within the profession.

One model already exists in Canada. In British Columbia, as in Scotland, a college of teachers, not a government ministry, regulates the profession. Like so many aspects of political life in that province, ideology explains much of the genesis of a new regulatory body for teachers.[8] In 1988, in a move to undercut the role of the provincial teachers' union, the Social Credit government created a college of teachers to regulate entry into the profession and advise on teacher training and competency standards. Five of the twenty-member body are appointed by the government and faculties of education, but the remainder are teachers, creating a balance of interest between professional and public interest.

Given the imperative for national standards in education, a college of teachers could set national standards of teaching and, in the process, dismantle unnecessary barriers that now impede the mobility of qualified teachers. Ideally, a college of teachers would be a new vehicle to foster a stronger relationship between faculties of education, employers and practising teachers. At present, such relationships are ad hoc, based more on successful personal relationships than a philosophical commitment to placing teachers and schools in contact with the outside world. Ending the antagonism of "them" and "us" is essential to ensuring a more informed public debate about education.

With new status, however, come new levels of responsibility and accountability. If the power of certification of teachers is to be transferred from government to the profession, then society will look for a *quid pro quo*, a guarantee that the teaching profession will not become aloof and unresponsive to public concerns and complaints, as other self-governing professional groups have often been. Teachers deserve a new level of support and respect if they are to help Canadians improve their education system, but in return teachers must demonstrate a new openness and respect for the other stakeholders in education.

High Standards for Teaching

The first task of a college of teachers would be to define national standards for entry to the profession. This exercise would require careful analysis of the professional competencies both inside and outside the classroom expected of today's teachers and a realistic appraisal of what should be expected of the teacher as he or she enters the profession. If certification of teachers were based on demonstrated competency, rather than on time spent in university, the faculties of education could then begin to redefine their own programs with an eye to these standards. As things stand, no one group has any clear responsibility for defining the educational and training needs of a teacher.

As professionals, teachers can be expected to make an ongoing commitment to their careers, and the idea of a teaching certificate that is renewable every five years should be given serious consideration. However, demonstrations of professional education and growth could take several forms. A college of teachers would play an important role in establishing standards both for teaching and for areas of special responsibility; for example, educational management (for principals), professional development and training (for assisting faculties of education with student teachers), and curriculum development (for developing new or innovative programs) should be recognized specialties demanding formal education and training at the university level.

Professional Growth Opportunities for Teachers

One of the success stories in Canadian education is the development of co-op education, which allows students to combine their studies with work experience. The same opportunities should be given to teachers. The demands on a teacher are enormous and emotionally draining, so that even the best professionals have difficulty maintaining their enthusiasm for the job over time. The risk of boredom, repetitiveness and cynicism runs high for those who remain in the classroom. The changing ethnic and racial mix of the classroom, conflicts over what should be taught and confusion over education goals all complicate the work of the teacher. To some, teaching may look easy and even undemanding, but it is a difficult, complex undertaking at which only the best truly succeed. Moreover, professional advancement is attained by leaving the classroom, through promotion and significantly higher pay for school board administrators and ministry officials.

One way to keep good teachers in the classroom is to allow them time off, without loss of seniority, to work for a brief stint in industry or the non-profit sector or as private entrepreneurs. The key condition attached to such a co-op program is that it be tied to the teacher's professional development in the classroom. Those who now criticize teachers, especially in business, have a responsibility to help teachers learn from professionals in their subject area or specialty. One untapped opportunity for business partnerships would give teachers hands-on experience in an industrial setting. Some U.S. companies, for example, pay science teachers to work in their labs for a brief period before they return to the classroom.

A major sore point between teachers and the public is the status of professional development days. The public views these half-day and full-day breaks, negotiated in all teacher contracts, as unwarranted disruptions during the school year. They have become especially inconvenient in an era when the mother, the parent who traditionally stayed home, is out in the workforce. The need for teachers to receive paid opportunities for professional growth is clear but this need should not be met at the expense of the needs of children in the classroom. In future, professional days should be moved outside the regular school schedule, with teachers paid accordingly. The issue here is not to penalize teachers; they need every kind of public support and encouragement for doing a difficult job. More flexible staffing in schools — in our model, the exclusive responsibility of each school council — will enable teachers to receive the professional growth opportunities they need with no disruption to the school program. In addition, the benefits of professional days — or their equivalent — must be explained and assessed in ways that the public can understand.

Teachers' Responsibility and Accountability

Under the traditional "factory model" of education, workers unionized in response to owners unwilling to pay better wages and managers resistant to improving working conditions. Collective agreements negotiated in such a confrontational atmosphere inevitably have led to strict terms and conditions that constrain the staffing and operation of schools. Those with a big stake in education, the students, parents and employers, have had little opportunity for feedback on the implications of those negotiations.

The new economic realities create an opportunity to modify the educational hierarchy in ways that reward co-operation, not confrontation. In the current climate, teachers' unions and school boards or ministries can ill afford to fight over contracts because there is neither the money nor the political support for even modest wage hikes. Like medical and legal fees, teachers' salaries should be negotiated at the provincial level — as already occurs in some provinces — thereby eliminating one current role of many school boards.

Changes in the way schools are governed and the development of national standards for teachers would contribute to a new evaluation of the worth of the classroom teacher, relative to that of other education professionals. As things are, salaries reflect the administrative and supervisory hierarchy that is typical of a factory-model education system. In a reinvented system, the salary structure might reflect a different set of values and priorities; for example, the administrative position of principal (teacher) might be matched equally with other positions of special responsibility such as curriculum leadership or supervision of student teachers.

If teachers want a larger voice in what happens in the classroom, they must be better prepared than they are at present to explain what they do and why. The issue of performance assessment, of course, is a political minefield because no one is sure what teachers should be held accountable for. "Any occupation group...which aspires to the status of a profession must have fair but effective ways of dealing with serious complaints about the performance of its members," the New Brunswick education inquiry observed. "There is a widespread perception that teaching does not."[9] Despite the potential difficulties involved in judging performance, some teacher organizations in the United States are working with education officials to develop acceptable yardsticks. In North Carolina, for instance, teachers in one school district accepted a district plan that ties their pay increases to success in meeting individual and school-wide performance goals. In Kentucky also, teachers and all education professionals accept responsibility for meeting a school's targets.

Teachers have legitimate concerns about performance reviews and other subjective assessments that discriminate on the basis of unfair criteria. The challenge, however, is to devise standards acceptable to teachers and the public alike. As schools become more democratic, collaborative working environments, teachers, principals and the outside community must reward team work and innovation. Just as teachers have standards for evaluating student performance, so too there is scope for evaluations of teachers.

The public and the teaching profession have to look at ways to require poor teachers to improve their performance or leave the profession and, equally, to reward the successful. With the cross-currents now buffeting the profession, teachers and the public have a shared responsibility to resolve the ambiguities that undermine good teaching and effective learning. What is missing today, and is much needed for the future, is a forthright discussion about ideas and practices that will help teachers, as professionals, to do their job even better and that will reward them appropriately for doing so.

Innovation in Schools

If education is failing to learn from its own experience, no amount of university upgrading or national standard setting will help if innovative ideas are stifled or hidden in one classroom. A few years ago, the parents of First Avenue Public School in Ottawa — a school with an excellent reputation in an affluent area of the city — presented the school with its first computer. In due course the children in one Grade 4 class were excited to learn its secrets. By the end of the year, they were all quite adept at booting it up, playing a few games, and using some of the available software. With anticipation, they returned to school in Grade 5 to learn more about the computer. But their Grade 5 teacher knew nothing of computers nor, as they found out a year later, did their Grade 6 teacher. They never saw the computer in class again. The Grade 4 teacher, when challenged for a reason, pointed out that he had no authority to teach his colleagues to use computers and that there was nothing that could be done. His expertise was carefully locked away so that children in only one grade of six in the school had access to it.

Such a situation is typical of education. In her study of science education in an elementary school in Nova Scotia, researcher Mary Schoeneberger found that few teachers taught any science and what expertise in this field existed in the school remained in the same few classrooms. Of one of the few teachers who did teach some science, she wrote:

> Among his colleagues, Mr. Blake is recognized as the "science person" in the school. Mr. Blake suggests he is perceived this way because he is trained in science and had worked in science-related areas prior to becoming a teacher. Most teachers, however, do not use Mr. Blake as a resource person on a regular basis although they know he is available if they wish to approach him. Because a classroom teacher serving as a resource person can only influence and be helpful but cannot demand, the onus for change remains with each individual teacher.[10]

For others in the school, as with many in the community, science was seen as "a little added frill."[11] In the present context, Mr. Blake's story illustrates well the reason that science in elementary schools has advanced so slowly, despite policies from all the provincial ministries of education.

Innovation, in computers, science, or any other aspect of education, occurs with snail-like slowness in schools. There are many reasons for this but one of the most significant is lack of leadership. Principals are the most influential people in creating a school culture and a principal who is not inclined to support innovation will provide few rewards for teachers to try new things or to spread their expertise around. By contrast, a principal who wants to see an innovation take root in his or her school can take many steps to ensure that it does.

Unfortunately, the entrepreneurial principal who sees in every challenge an opportunity and who is prepared to take risks (of bureaucratic problems for himself or herself) in the interests of the students is all too rare. There are few rewards and many obstacles for teachers and principals who are innovative and creative, and thus change, when it occurs at all, occurs very slowly indeed.

This is the culture that must be changed, and local control is an important step in ensuring that it does. A principal who is appointed by the community and who is given a clear mandate for change can work to achieve results, knowing he or she has the support of the community. Local control is important but it is not enough. Principals, like teachers, must be trained to focus on achieving results for students as their primary goal. Then, with an appropriate structure and the necessary skills, the principal can be held accountable for delivering results.

Principals must be curriculum and instructional leaders first and administrators second. As long as there is a massive bureaucratic hierarchy above them, this priority is almost bound to be reversed. With local control and a global vision, schools can be expected to be as innovative as necessary to achieve results.

Research and Development

Ideas are the key to growth in any enterprise. Public education is in dire need of more research and development to help teachers adjust to the new realities of the classroom, to an emerging information-dependent society and to the new budgetary strait-jacket. Like the debate over teachers as professionals, the discussion about education research is marred by a suspicion and contempt for "experts." Innovations in teaching and learning come and go like fads and, when the "new" ideas are cloaked in obscure language, parents grow understandably restive about being patronized.

Unfortunately, little comprehensive information is available about the extent of education research and development in Canada. Even in the United States, which typically outperforms Canada in spending on R&D, spending on new technology is only about $1,000 per employee, compared to $7,000 to $20,000 in other sectors and up to $300,000 in high-tech industry, according to U.S. education critic Lewis Perelman. The ratio for education drops to about $100, if the ratio uses students instead of teachers. The U.S. Office of Technology Assessment, a research arm of the Congress, estimates that the United States spends only 0.025 per cent of the total education budget on R&D, well below that of Germany at 0.2 per cent, and Britain at 0.18 per cent.[12]

What the U.S. data show is that education still relies on nineteenth century technology to train students for the twenty-first century. The same is true for Canada. What is needed is a revolution in ideas, to change the way society and schools think about the education experience, with a sharper focus on learning and results. Research and development should be harnessed to support learning on all rungs of the education ladder.

As a cornerstone for building public confidence in education, research can take many forms. The increasingly multicultural, multiracial character of schools should stimulate *basic research* into how children learn and the factors that inhibit or accelerate the process. Research is also needed in Canada on such issues as mastery learning — how to promote and facilitate student achievement of real competencies and how to assess it; effective schools — what makes some schools more effective and others less so; and co-operative learning — how to stimulate students to work together in the classroom and then how to assess the outcome fairly and effectively.

By contrast, *applied research* could examine alternatives for teaching the "new basics" and evaluating student performance. On such controversial issues as reading methods and testing, in particular, researchers have an opportunity — and a responsibility — to inform parents and others about the menu of options required for effective learning. Canadians can ill afford to become trapped by ideological wars in education. Applied research can also examine how to harness technology to assist learning in the classroom.

A third type of inquiry, *policy research*, is needed to guide the renewal of education institutions and goals. In this regard, both levels of government, universities and the private sector have a bigger role to play in fostering a healthy public debate about education choices. In this day of tight budgets, one important policy question would ask how the achievement of students is related to the cost of providing their education.

Who should undertake this research? At present there are two principal groups of educational researchers in Canada. The first group is located in university faculties of education and undertakes research in conjunction with the members' roles as teacher educators. Because of this dual role, and the central place of teacher education to the work of the faculty, research is often undertaken as an add-on activity on a very small scale. This is compounded by the relatively small budget of the Social Sciences and Humanities Research Council and the fact that education must compete with all the other humanities and social sciences for this research funding. Despite this, some outstanding research in education has emerged from Canadian universities over the years. But the overall amount is still small. To change this would require substantially larger amounts of support for educational R&D to be made available.

The second group of researchers in the education field in Canada is attached to ministries of education and to some school boards. These people tend to undertake evaluation or assessment projects and research relevant to current policy questions. There is rarely co-ordinated connection among such researchers or between this group and the university-based research community.

There are no private-sector or federal government researchers in the education field. Also, unlike in the United States and several other countries, there are no national research institutes or think-tanks dedicated to educational research. In the United States, the federal government supports a series of regional "laboratories" of educational R&D. In Britain, the National Foundation for Educational Research performs an essentially parallel function. The Canadian federal government could usefully establish a national research centre to undertake basic, applied and policy research in all areas of education, and a special fund to support research by scholars elsewhere in Canada, as was suggested by Stuart Smith in his recent study of university teaching.[13]

To have impact, research and development must be widely disseminated and discussed by those in a position to use it, in this case teachers. Researchers must be encouraged to describe the results of their work in language that people can understand, and teachers and other educational professionals must learn how to interpret research results and apply them in the context of their own schools. To date, schools in Canada do not have a good track record of keeping up to date with research from around the world. Given new information technologies, this process should become much easier and, given more encouragement to innovate, schools can be expected to seek out and use research results more frequently.

Finally, teachers should be encouraged to participate more in research themselves. Schools should be places for inquiry where teachers and researchers work together to learn more about teaching and learning. Breaking down the barriers that tend to separate researchers from teachers is needed in order that the skills and insights of both may be brought to bear on the important questions of students' teaching and learning.

As a country, Canada has been reluctant to make the political and financial investment in research and innovation in many sectors of the economy. Canadians are now paying the price in plant closings and loss of competitive advantage to countries that put a premium on ideas. Canada still has a chance to learn from its mistakes — and its successes. In distance and co-op education, for example, Canadian expertise is recognized internationally. That capacity for innovation must now be extended more systematically so that all schools and teachers can fulfil their potential to learn from experience.

Conclusion

As practitioners in the learning business, teachers must themselves become learners and schools must be the laboratories in which the arts and sciences of education are acquired and used. Reinventing education is in an essential sense an intellectual activity. If schools are to become places for effective learning by students, they must set examples for the students of the discipline demanded of a lively intellectual life.

As long as schools remain places where teachers mindlessly "implement" rules and policies developed by others, then students will, equally mindlessly, learn to behave in the same way. But creativity begets creativity and critical inquiry is born in an environment of critical inquiry. If society is serious about the higher level intellectual activity that the new basics suggest, then the environment in which students and teachers work together must be a model of such intellectual activity.

To be true to this new vision, teachers need to be recognized as true professionals with the autonomy that the name implies, innovation must become the watchword for every school and research and development must be part of every school. Taking responsibility for their schools places the onus on all Canadians to ensure that this vision becomes reality.

Chapter 9

A Call to Arms

*C*anadians *have typically* treated problems in education as
somebody else's fault or as someone else's responsibility to fix. The
criticism and the complacency are equally corrosive. The bleak evaluation of schools by many critics is as misleading as their simplistic
prescription for a return to "the basics." Those who only blame the
system fail to appreciate how schools have had to respond to the
complex demands of an increasingly diverse student body and now
must adapt further to deal with the uncertain demands of the future.
Equally, those who believe that nothing needs to be done to
improve Canada's schools have no grounds for their complacency.
Historically, Canadians have prospered as a nation in the belief that
being "pretty good" was good enough, an illusion shattered by the
economic upheaval and uncertainty in the 1990s. The perceptions of
criticism and complacency are wrong and, if accepted as common
wisdom, will condemn us to repeat the failures of the past.

It is high time to pursue more constructive lines of inquiry and action. The public can no longer watch from the sidelines, quietly stewing. Parents, students, teachers, employers and, indeed, governments are not getting what they need from the education system. But in tackling the challenges in education, individuals, groups and institutions must come to grips with the complexities of education and demonstrate a new willingness to examine their own preconceptions. Otherwise, the needed reforms will be left, by default, to the educational insiders or to single interests, both of whom are intent on imposing their own, often narrow agendas.

The traditional assumptions underpinning the Canadian social contract in education are increasingly being challenged. The erosion of this contract is evident in the public's pervasive mistrust of teachers and schools — and they of the public. The fragmentation of families, the rise of regional interests, the downward shift of fiscal obligations from one level of government to the next all have taken their toll on education. Increasingly, Canadians define their differences by language, religion and geography; they are less sure about what they share as a nation or, indeed, as a community. No wonder the public is confused and often angry about what they see happening at school.

Canadians can chart a new course. It begins with a recognition that education is everyone's responsibility. This outlook rests on three simple truths. First, no one, including the schools, can do the job alone. Second, the traditional response to Canadian problems — more money — is neither politically nor economically viable unless it results in demonstrable improvements in the system. Third, there is no single formula for success; a diverse mix of solutions will be crafted through commitment and compromise by all those dedicated to helping students and schools to do their best.

School reform, as others have noted, is not a spectator sport.[1] Increasingly, parents, employers, teachers and politicians realize that education cannot be viewed as a political blood sport between critics and defenders of the status quo. Canadians need to work together to resolve the dilemmas and conflicts that bedevil education.

The most fundamental dilemma is how to reconcile the imperatives of equity and excellence. Public education is supposed to serve all comers, an institutional mirror of the diversity of the nation. Yet schools are also expected to turn out high calibre graduates who can compete against their peers in Japan, Europe and the United States. Canadians typically expect public education to shoulder most of the responsibility for the intellectual, emotional and moral development of students, criticizing the schools when they fall short. Canadians expect schools to provide vocational options for young people but, at the same time, as parents and employers, they put a premium on university as the ticket for success. The public pays lip service to the idea of success for every student but fails to address the barriers created by poverty and family breakdown. Schools are expected to turn out graduates able to think for themselves, yet the rigid structure of education condemns them to spend a dozen years in institutions that reward conformity. In their multiple roles, schools are expected to resolve conflicts for which even Canadian society does not have answers yet.

A resolution of these dilemmas is only the first step in mapping new routes to excellence for all students. It is time, therefore, to move to the politics of solutions in education. It will not be easy. Excellence in education has always been a challenge, although it has usually implied rewarding winners and leaving losers behind. Now a much greater challenge confronts Canadians: to strike a better balance between the important goal of educational excellence and the equally ambitious goal of equity, with its implicit commitment that no one be forgotten by the school system. Claiming that the system is dedicated to both excellence and equity, while not demonstrating achievement of either, will no longer do. A new social contract is needed for education, based on new understanding about how children learn; more flexible approaches to how schools can best support and assess learning; new structures and technologies designed to meet the challenges of the twenty-first century; and a new commitment on the part of all members of society to take responsibility for Canada's schools.

Reforms in Other Jurisdictions

Canada is not alone in its desire to improve the education system. Most industrial countries, including the United States and Britain, are reassessing their school systems in light of changing social and economic conditions. Although the school reform innovations of other countries will be of little help if we are uncertain about our own goals for education, they do offer some lessons and insights.

Among the American states, Kentucky ranks near the bottom in its proportion of the population who graduate from high school. Determined to end its backward status, Kentucky has undergone one of the most radical education reform programs in the United States. Faced with a 1989 court decision, which ruled the state's entire system of common schools unconstitutional on the grounds that educational resources and, thus, opportunities to learn were distributed inequitably, Kentucky legislators were given until April 1990 to devise a brand new system. The reforms turned the education system on its head, replacing a rule-bound bureaucracy with decentralized decision making and giving political power to parents and others at the local level. The new system relies on carrot-and-stick incentives, with local schools given more freedom so long as they meet newly defined state educational goals.[2]

Although the changed legislative framework for the new Kentucky school system was in place within a year of the court decision, by late 1992 only one-third of the 176 local community citizen groups — intended as the real agents of change — were in place and school boards were fighting their loss of political power in the courts. Despite the efforts of state-wide citizens' groups, business and state government, voter turnout among parents for the school council elections still is low. Supporters of the Kentucky reforms have not lost faith in their campaign to raise educational standards and expectations in the state. However, Kentucky teaches the lessons that there are no quick fixes in school reform and that time and persistence are required to build consensus at both state and local levels.

New York State has taken a less dramatic route to reform than Kentucky. In 1991, Governor Mario Cuomo, supported by representatives of business, parents' groups, teachers' unions and local school districts, unveiled "A New Compact for Learning," which seeks to clarify roles and responsibilities for all the constituents in education from the state to the student.[3] Unlike Kentucky's new legal framework, New York seeks to promote a greater degree of commitment by all players, especially those at the local level, to make the existing system work better. The state has pledged itself to be more explicit about what should be learned while giving schools and school districts more freedom to determine how these goals should be attained. Without reallocating formal decision-making responsibilities, the state uses the "New Compact" as a framework for engaging parents and community members to play their full part in the education system. In effect, New York's reforms are predicated on the assumption that the existing structure needs to be improved but not replaced. The New York State experience demonstrates that much can be accomplished without formal, statutory reorganization of the school system, since the very notion of a "compact" implies a political and social consensus. As in Kentucky, the success of the New York reforms will be judged on how well parents and the community respond to the challenge to become full participants in decisions affecting the life of schools. The Commissioner of Education, Dr. Thomas Sobol, and the staff of the state education department are spending time and effort working with local parents and community groups, helping them develop the skills and knowledge required to become a more potent force within the school system. In New York, officials of the State Education Department are taking the message to all parts of the state, convening parent and community workshops and providing new local and regional forums for citizens to deliberate about education.

Between the models of Kentucky and New York is a third example of American reform. California and several other states have legislated the establishment of "charter schools." Under California legislation, for example, parents and teachers are permitted to set up their own schools free from some of the traditional bureaucratic rules laid down for public schools.[4] In effect, the state is creating a new breed of alternative, quasi-independent schools. These "charter" schools are allowed to offer programs and teaching methods of their own design, especially for low-achieving students — in return for less bureaucratic interference from the state. In its reforms, California is sending a new message about what counts in the 1990s: results. The state appears to be less interested in whether these schools follow a strict set of procedures than in how well they perform in meeting the state's education goals. The California lesson shows the potential for increasing diversity and choice within the overall framework of a public education system that is still, for the most part, centrally operated.

In England and Wales, where élite independent schools and less prosperous "state" schools have traditionally operated side by side, recent government reforms have centralized some decisions and decentralized others. Even as the government has introduced a national curriculum and standards, London has given local communities more control over education. Once again, the political losers are school boards, known there as local education authorities. Under the Education Reform Act of 1988 and the Education (Schools) Act of 1992, schools can opt out of being managed by their local education authorities so long as 75 percent of parents agree to the change.[5] As in the United States, the idea is to give parents choice among more alternative schools and learning styles within the framework of defined national goals. Recognizing that not all schools are ready to take on the responsibilities involved in self-government, the education minister envisions a ten-year phase-in before the majority of schools opt out. The lesson from Britain is two-fold: first, gradualism is key to reforms in political power and, second, there must be a process through which citizens can become engaged and clear benefits outlined to encourage their engagement. In the British case, the promise of direct local control over their schools is expected to be a powerful incentive for communities to take their responsibility for education seriously.

A Made-in-Canada Approach

Neither as committed to individual rights as the Americans, nor as class-conscious as the British, Canadians must hammer out compromises on school reform that reflect their own history, society and economy. The strong provincial and relatively weak federal presence in education, the increasingly multicultural character of the urban areas and the particular and changing mix of the national economy all dictate that Canada adapt the best ideas to suit conditions here.

In addition, changes in political structure and decision making cannot be imposed on schools and communities; they must be undertaken with a clear political mandate. In the past, educational reform has usually been attempted in a top-down management style, without sufficient regard for those on the receiving end of the changes. Apart from the inherent inefficiencies of this approach, Canadians are tired of deals and accords that are negotiated by political élites and that they are then expected to accept. In education, perhaps more than anywhere else in public life, people want to have their own say because the consequences of success and failure are so high.

Issues of control, curriculum standards and testing must be addressed by all Canadians through honest debate and deliberation on education. Such discussion must take place at local, provincial and national levels in a co-ordinated fashion that promotes consensus building. It must involve all those in the education process, both insiders and those currently on the outside, parents, employers, university and college faculty, and students themselves. And this deliberative process must inform those in a position to make decisions.

There is already a precedent for this kind of deliberation. In 1983, the Science Council of Canada convened conferences in every province and territory to discuss the state of science education in elementary and secondary schools. Those two-day conferences, attended by a full range of local interest groups and informed by the Council's research in the field, had a double impact: they enabled the Council to state with confidence in its final report that a national consensus existed concerning eight specific directions for the future of science education,[6] and they ensured that there was a group of people in each province and territory ready and, in some cases, already moving to implement the desired directions.

However, there are prerequisites for such deliberations to be successful.[7] First, a broad cross-section of the community must take part, supported by an environment that enables them to build consensus. One-sided consultations that lead to a predetermined path or, alternatively, debates over theoretical principles removed from a policy context are no substitute for effective debate and discussion.

Second, there must be a complete sharing of information about the education system. Canadians want to be able to judge, more easily than they can now, what is good, bad and indifferent about their schools. The educational establishment has an obligation to speak a language the public understands so as to dispel the myths and superficial assumptions that now preclude a full exploration of the issues. For its part, the public must recognize — as too few people do now — that education is a complex business. Parents and employers need to understand what factors explain why it is that some students learn faster than others —- and how they can help the others catch up.

Finally, there must be real options for practical action to form the substance of the deliberative process, accompanied by a commitment to follow through on the results. In this, as elsewhere, the provinces can show leadership; for example, the New Brunswick education inquiry purposely declined to draft a "mission statement" on education for the province, rightly arguing that it was a matter for the citizens of the province. The minister of education then brought in interest groups from across the province to draft the statement. Such an exercise, however, will be worth nothing if the government and the public pay only lip service to the goals. The goals must have enough impact to ensure that the system demonstrates increased accountability and integrity.

A made-in-Canada approach to school reform must address the six key areas outlined in this book: how power is distributed; how schools operate; how to set clear and achievable goals; how to measure the results; how to share responsibilities for education; and how to ensure the education system sustains itself in fresh and innovative ways. Whatever the final components of a new arrangement on education, they should meet the tests of clarity, integrity and accountability — the touchstones of a reinvented system. These tests should apply at all levels of the system, from the family to the federal government.

1. Redistribute Power

A redistribution of power in education is essential. Parents, students, teachers and employers all must assume more effective roles in the decision-making process. But any structural overhaul of the education system must also pass the "Titanic test." In other words, the public must be assured that breaking the insiders' hold on the educational agenda does more than shuffle the proverbial deck chairs on the ship. Significant improvements in education quality and performance will be possible only with a new system of checks and balances: more local control over some issues would be offset by more central control over other issues. At the provincial and national levels, for example, Canadians would participate in defining common, publicly understood goals for education, with standards for measuring student and school achievement. Meanwhile, elected school councils of parents, students and teachers would have a direct voice in decisions about the curriculum and other local issues so long as they met well-articulated standards at the provincial and national levels. Under such a redistribution of power, school boards would lose their political authority, though they would likely continue to exist in an administrative or support capacity. Meanwhile, the role of ministries of education would be significantly reduced because school program decisions would now be made at the local level. The cost savings from a slimmed-down bureaucracy would be ploughed back into the schools.

Even with political will and legislative change, however, these new democratic institutions in education will not emerge overnight. Indeed, local autonomy is no panacea; that much is clear from reforms elsewhere. Parents, students, teachers, employers and others will need training and facilitation to learn to talk to — and listen to — each other so as to acknowledge their differences and agree on shared goals. Moreover, increased local autonomy must not be seen as a convenient way for a new set of élites or interest groups to dominate the agenda. Despite these caveats, parents, teachers and the entire community have a responsibility to help build schools with character, schools that stand for something, schools that demonstrate the attributes of flexibility, diversity and inclusivity — the very values many Canadians espouse for their children.

At the local level, schools are, literally, where the action is; they must also be where the decisions are made in the best interests of their students. The appeal of local school democracy is that it allows members of the community to become real, not rhetorical, partners with the school. Teachers, parents and communities can start immediately to elect community school councils to begin deliberating over future directions for their school in a co-operative rather than a confrontational mode. When the time comes for such councils to take on full responsibility for their schools, those with the most experience of working together will be in the best position to operate effectively. School principals can take immediate leadership here in reaching out to the community throughout the year.

Beyond these informal changes in school attitudes, the provinces will need to enact legislation to provide for local councils to have real political power. An important first step in this direction is for political parties to endorse fundamental restructuring of schools as part of their policy platforms. In Ontario, the implications of redistributing power should be explored by the government's proposed commission on education. The key to introducing both formal and informal changes is the political endorsement of individual Canadians for a redistribution of power in education.

2. Redefine Schools

Schools must rededicate themselves to the enterprise of learning. The task sounds easy, but it is in fact extraordinarily difficult given the complexity of schools. The use of time, the grouping of students, the management of staff and teaching assignments, the application of technology and the means of student assessment must all be reorganized to enhance the student's opportunity to learn.

To accommodate the individual differences and the heterogeneous nature of today's school populations, Canadians must be prepared to go beyond the traditional ways in which students have been grouped, learning scheduled, and resources distributed. In the past, the relative lack of technology and administrative considerations have constrained the ways in which schools have provided for learning; for example, the standard staffing model used in schools throughout the country sees one teacher working with about thirty students at a time throughout the school day. Other models, as the German experiments at Köln-Holweide demonstrate, allow for flexible groupings of teachers and para-professionals who work with students and use technology in the support of effective learning. Local autonomy is a key to unlocking this possibility, because school councils would have the right to introduce measures that meet the needs of their own community.

Beyond these institutional considerations, schools must dismantle the bureaucratic walls that separate students and teachers from the communities they serve. Students can learn in many ways and from many different people in a variety of settings. As the co-op education movement has shown, effective learning can take place outside the classroom; schools need every encouragement to discover the potential for learning in their own communities. Principals can take the lead to reach out to community leaders who can support and advise on school programs and, as well, support teachers in exploring community resources for their own teaching. School councils, where these already exist, have the potential to assist in this process of community bridge building.

3. Clarify the Vision

Canadians have to clarify what it is they want from their schools — an exercise to be undertaken at all levels of the education system from school councils to new national agencies. Discussion must lead to action. If the public really wants the school system to turn out flexible, creative, adaptable learners, are they prepared to explore the alternative approaches needed to achieve that goal? How does the desire of some employers for the new type of learner square with the desire of other employers for graduates who do not question authority?

Above all, Canadians must make their expectations about outcomes realistic and achievable for every student. All students should be given the help they need to reach the desired standards before moving to the next stage of school and ultimately to graduation from high school. Employers, parents and others will have to recognize that some students will take longer to reach the standard than others. In return, the public will have greater assurance about the worth of a high school diploma.

The provinces have an opportunity to show significant leadership by joining forces with the federal government in the establishment of a Canadian Educational Standards Council and an associated testing service. If the provinces fail to co-operate, the federal government should go it alone since these new national bodies could be designed so as not to infringe on provincial powers. Federal-provincial co-operation in education is long overdue. The standards council would be made up of appointees from throughout the country, selected not from the bureaucracy but from the public at large, as a signal of the importance of involving everyone in the process.

4. Measure Success

Canadians need systematic, reliable and fair ways of measuring results for individuals, schools and the system as a whole. The assessment must be credible, publicly available and communicated in an understandable fashion. Issues of testing and evaluation cannot be treated simplistically as they are now; everyone needs to understand what kinds of tests work best and for what desired ends. Teachers and the experts in evaluation will need to educate the public as never before so that they all can put a realistic value on test results.

At present, provinces vary enormously in the degree and manner in which the results of education are assessed. The task of educational assessment is a complex one technically as well as politically. But there is considerable expertise in Canada on which to draw to ensure that evaluation is no longer a patchwork quilt of standards across the country. The Canadian Educational Testing Service we propose would focus the political commitment and the technical expertise to address specific provincial needs and ensure that Canadians from coast to coast have confidence in the results of their investment in education. To create this service, the provinces and the federal government will have to show a new readiness to co-operate.

At the local level, there is much that can be done immediately. Teachers and schools can resolve to make clear the achievement measures they use, explaining without jargon how they assess student progress. No legislation or changes in policy are required to bring about more open communication between school and home. Schools can begin by demonstrating their commitment to talk unambiguously to parents; in turn, parents have an obligation to take a balanced view of school issues, recognizing that their point of view is not the only valid one.

5. Share Responsibility

Education is too important to be left exclusively to the professionals. On their own, schools cannot do the difficult job expected of them. However, partnerships in the full sense of the word have yet to materialize. In theory, parents, employers and other members of the community have a nominal say in educational affairs, but in reality the level of involvement is superficial. It must be deepened. The public needs to reassert ownership of education with a new charter of roles and responsibilities in which everyone has a meaningful part to play.

Families must do their bit to support their children by sending a clear message about educational excellence. Children who come to school ready to learn have the best shot at success. Like society itself, parents can be good or poor role models; they can support the work ethic and work co-operatively with schools on such issues as homework and study habits or they can fail to play their part. Canadians can take a direct lesson from Chinese and Japanese families in providing children with study areas at home and making studying as much a part of normal family life as other activities. Families also need help to do their job well. Some schools already have developed "parent education" programs to assist parents with the task of supporting their children's learning at home and these could become the norm in all schools. Other community agencies, such as libraries, service clubs and cultural organizations, could also make this a focus for direct action.

Members of the business community can play their part, too, without waiting for legislative or policy change — many are already doing so. They can institute family leaves for parents, encourage their employees to visit schools, accept students and teachers in co-op placements and help schools acquire new equipment. They can also work together through local chambers of commerce or, at the national level, through industrial associations and through organizations such as the Conference Board of Canada, in communicating to schools their recognition of the value of the work of teachers and schools.

Universities and colleges too often stay on the sidelines, preferring to criticize than to help. However, some post-secondary institutions recognize that they have a stake in school success. Universities and colleges must do even more to work with local school systems to support learning, to assist teachers with continuing education and resources for teaching and to encourage students to stay in school. Today's high school students are tomorrow's university and college freshmen. If only in its own self-interest, the post-secondary education sector can support schools in achieving the goal of ensuring excellence for all.

6. Learn from Experience

Schools must become institutions that put a premium on learning. Not only must they focus on students' learning, they must also become more effective and intellectually stimulating places in which to work. This can happen in three ways: first, through higher expectations for teachers and improved provision of teacher education at all levels; second, through a new commitment to innovation in the delivery of school programs; and, third, through increased research and development in support of education in Canada.

Present structures and attitudes in the education system impede opportunities to learn from experience. Structurally, education must adopt the "Moosehead principle." Until recently, because of interprovincial trade barriers in Canada, this Maritime brew was more famous in the United States than in the rest of Canada. Now, thanks to the gradual dismantling of internal trade barriers in Canada, Moosehead is sold across Canada. The same liberation principle should be applied to education in Canada: remove the artificial barriers and promote the free flow of good ideas. In many communities across the country, there is much that is positive, inspiring and largely unrecognized in the work of teachers, schools and, above all, the students themselves. These initiatives must be reinforced, recognized and rewarded because they show what is possible even under difficult circumstances.

The necessary reinforcement, recognition and rewards are expressions of a new attitude towards innovation and intellectual entrepreneurship in Canada's schools. At present, too many teachers play safe professionally knowing that this will never hurt them, even if it never causes excitement or enthusiasm for learning among students. Others, often unsupported and unrecognized, are the risk takers who go the extra mile for their students, who will do anything to ensure a child's success and who live for the love of learning. Great teachers need to be recognized for their successes with children rather than for their longevity or their capacity never to offend their superiors. School councils and principals can show leadership in signalling to all teachers what is considered valuable in their school.

Conclusion

Canadians have an opportunity to engage in a new type of nation building through their schools. The effort begins with a more constructive conversation about roles, rights and responsibilities in education and in recognition that school reform is a shared enterprise. By moving beyond the repairs and rebuilding efforts of the past, Canadians can transform the education system in ways that reinvent how schools work.

These reforms require a new level of commitment by individuals, institutions and interest groups to take responsibility for their schools. Georges Clemenceau once said that war was too important to be left to the generals. Likewise, education cannot be left to those who run the system. All Canadians must play their part. Governments, both provincial and federal, have their role to play in legislating new structures that will reshape the system in a way more suited to the coming century than the last. But all Canadians, both as individuals and as members of groups, are the ones who will ultimately make the difference. The effort will be repaid many times over as citizens create reasons to renew confidence in the education system. The assignment awaits completion. The pay-off and final grade are for the next generation.

Notes

Chapter 1: Voices in Conflict

1. The Angus Reid/Southam News Poll, *Making the Grade: Public Opinion on Education in Canada* (Toronto: Angus Reid Group, 1993).

2. In this opinion, Harold Lockhart is not alone. According to the latest OISE survey of public attitudes towards education, 55 per cent of Ontarians would like to see increased spending on elementary and secondary schools, a higher proportion than in all but one previous survey (David W. Livingstone et al., *Public Attitudes Towards Education*, 1992, Ninth OISE Survey. [Toronto: Ontario Institute for Studies in Education, 1993]).

3. Statistics Canada, *School Leavers Survey* (Ottawa: Statistics Canada, 1991), p. 2.

4. British Columbia Ministry of Education, private communication.

5. A.J.C. King and M.J. Peart, *Teachers in Canada: Their Work and Quality of Life* (Ottawa: Canadian Teachers' Federation, 1992), p. 121.

6. Premier's Council Report, *People and Skills in the New Global Economy* (Toronto: Government of Ontario, 1990), p. 30.

7. According to Statistics Canada (*School Leavers Survey*, op. cit.), as many as half of all drop-outs return to school at some point, and over 5 per cent of all high school graduates had "dropped out" at some stage.

8. International Assessment of Educational Progress, *Learning Mathematics* (Princeton, N.J.: Educational Testing Service, 1992), p. 12.

9. Statistics Canada, *Advance Statistics of Education, 1992-93*. Statistics Canada Daily Release, September 1, 1992.

10. Economic Council of Canada, *A Lot to Learn: Education and Training in Canada* (Ottawa: Supply and Services Canada, 1992), p. 7.

11. C.E. Ritchie, Address to the Canadian Association of University Business Officers, Winnipeg, June 15, 1992.

12. Canadian Federation of Independent Business, private communication, January 1993.

13. Government of Canada Prosperity Initiative, *Learning Well...Living Well*. Discussion Paper (Ottawa: Supply and Services Canada, 1991).

14. Lorne Bozinoff and André Turcotte, "Canadians Dissatisfied with the Education Children Are Receiving," *The Gallup Report* (September 7, 1992), Gallup Canada Inc.

15. Livingstone et al., op. cit.

Chapter 2: Education Under Stress

1. Lewis Perelman, *School's Out: Hyperlearning, the New Technology, and the End of Education* (New York: Morrow, 1992).

2. Robert S. Brown et al., *The 1991 Every Secondary Student Survey: Initial Findings* (Toronto: Toronto Board of Education, 1992).

3. Stephen Lewis, *Report on Race Relations in Ontario* (Toronto: Government of Ontario, 1992), p. 20.

4. Maureen Moore, "Women Parenting Alone," *Canadian Social Trends* (Winter 1987), p. 31.

5. Economic Council of Canada, *Good Jobs, Bad Jobs: Employment in the Service Economy* (Ottawa: Supply and Services Canada, 1990), p. 13.

6. Shona McKay, "Boys Club," *Report on Business Magazine* (September 1992), p. 37.

7. *Prosperity Through Innovation.* Report of the Task Force on Challenges in Science, Technology and Related Skills (Ottawa: Prosperity Secretariat, 1992), p. 4.

8. Michael Salter, "Blue Sky and Black Ink," *Report on Business Magazine* (September 1992), p. 69.

9. Donald Nightingale. Interview published in *Inside Guide* (November 1992), p. 35.

10. Conference Board of Canada, *Employability Skills Profile* (Ottawa: Conference Board of Canada, 1992).

11. Richard Belous, *Demographic Currents: Trends and Issues that Face the United States, the United Kingdom, and Canada.* Occasional Paper No. 7 (London: British North America Committee, 1991), p. 16.

12. David Osborne and Ted Gaebler, *Reinventing Government: How the Entrepreneurial Spirit Is Transforming the Public Sector* (New York: Addison Wesley, 1992), p. 25.

Chapter 3: Redistributing Power

1. David Osborne and Ted Gaebler, *Reinventing Government* (New York: Addison Wesley, 1992).

2. Department of Education and Science (England and Wales), *Choice and Diversity.* White Paper on Education (London: Her Majesty's Stationery Office, 1992).

3. Edward B. Fiske, *Smart Schools, Smart Kids: Why Do Some Schools Work?* (New York: Touchstone Books, 1991).

4. *America 2000: An Education Strategy Sourcebook* (Washington, D.C.: U.S. Government, 1991).

5. Eric Newell, Preface to *International Comparisons in Education — Curriculum, Values and Lessons* (Edmonton: Alberta Chamber of Resources and Alberta Education, 1991), p. i.

6. Steering Group on Prosperity, *Inventing Our Future* (Ottawa: Supply and Services Canada, 1992).

7. John D. Donahue, *The Privatisation Decision: Public Ends, Private Means* (New York: Basic Books, 1989), p. 7.

8. Organization for Economic Cooperation and Development, *Schools and Quality: An International Report* (Paris: OECD, 1989).

9. Chester Finn, "Why We Need Choice," in W.L. Boyd and H.J. Walberg (eds.), *Choice in Education: Potential and Problems* (Berkeley, CA: McCutcheon, 1990), p. 11.

10. See, for example, David Kirp, "What School Choice Really Means," *The Atlantic Monthly* (November 1992), pp. 119-32.

11. Bernard Shapiro, *Report on the Funding of Private Schools in Ontario* (Toronto: Ministry of Education, 1985).

Chapter 4: Redefining School

1. George Leonard, "The End of School," *The Atlantic Monthly* (May 1992), p. 25.

2. Theodore Sizer, "Reforming American Schools: Observations from the Coalition of Essential Schools." Presentation at the annual meeting of the American Educational Research Association, San Francisco, April 1992.

3. Lauren Resnick, "Learning In School and Out," *Educational Researcher* (December 1987), pp. 13-20.

4. Conference Board of Canada, *Employability Skills Profile: What Are Employers Looking For?* (Ottawa: Conference Board of Canada, 1992).

5. British Columbia Royal Commission on Education, *A Legacy for Learners* (Victoria: Queen's Printer for B.C., 1988).

6. International Assessment of Educational Progress, *Learning Science* (Princeton, N.J.: Educational Testing Service, 1992), p. 79.

7. Harold Stevenson and John Stigler, *The Learning Gap* (New York: Summit Books, 1992), p. 142.

8. Economic Council of Canada, *A Lot to Learn* (Ottawa: Supply and Services Canada, 1992), p. 15.

9. This account is based on Edward Fiske, *Smart Schools, Smart Kids: Why Do Some Schools Work?* (New York: Touchstone, 1992), p. 103.

10. Ibid., p. 93.

11. William E. Nothdurft, *SchoolWorks: Reinventing Public Schools to Create the Workforce of the Future* (Washington, D.C.: The Brookings Institution, 1989), p. 89.

12. Fiske, op. cit.

13. Fiske, op.cit., p. 147.

14. John Naisbitt, *Megatrends* (New York: Warner Books, 1982), p. 20.

15. Leonard, op.cit., p. 28.

Chapter 5: Clarifying the Vision

1. Ontario Ministry of Education, *The Common Curriculum, Grades 1 to 9* (Toronto: Government of Ontario, 1993).

2. Cindy Heine, *The School Answer Book: Citizens' Guide to Kentucky School Law* (Lexington, KY: Prichard Committee for Academic Excellence, 1992).

3. Ontario Ministry of Education, *The Common Curriculum*, op. cit.

4. Derek de Solla Price, *Little Science, Big Science and Beyond* (New York: Columbia University Press, 1990).

5. Economic Council of Canada, *Education and Training in Canada* (Ottawa: Supply and Services Canada, 1992), p. 23.

6. Science Council of Canada, *Science for Every Student: Educating Canadians for Tomorrow's World* (Ottawa: Supply and Services Canada, 1984).

7. For example: Robin Barrow, "So Much for the Mind" and John E. McPeck "Radwanski, Dropouts, and Thinking Skills" in Derek Allison and Jerry Paquette (eds.), *Reform and Relevance in Schooling: Dropouts, Destreaming and the Common Curriculum* (Toronto: OISE Press, 1991), pp. 9-18 and 83-91.

8. The Ontario government is citing the Radwanski report into drop-outs as the basis for many of its currently proposed reforms. Yet Radwanski came out strongly against the trend towards greater process objectives and the downgrading of subject-based content. See: George Radwanski, *Ontario Study of the Relevance of Education and the Issue of Dropouts* (Toronto: Ontario Ministry of Education, 1987).

9. The basic principles and standards for health care in Canada are set nationally while the administration of the health-care system remains under exclusive provincial jurisdiction, for example.

10. This proposal echoes one made by the Prosperity Initiative's Science and Technology Task Force, *Prosperity Through Innovation* (Ottawa: Conference Board of Canada, 1992).

11. The Committee on National Standards for Applied Science and Engineering is chaired by Graham Orpwood. Copies of the national standards may be obtained from the secretariat at 285 McLeod Street, Ottawa, K2P 1A1.

Chapter 6: Measuring Success

1. Council of Ministers of Education, Canada, *School Achievement Indicators Program: Memorandum of Understanding*, December 1991.

2. International Assessment of Educational Progress, *Learning Mathematics and Learning Science* (Princeton, NJ: Educational Testing Service, 1992).

3. Alberta Chamber of Resources, *International Comparisons in Education — Curriculum, Values and Lessons* (Edmonton: Alberta Chamber of Resources, 1991).

4. Ontario Ministry of Education, *Mathematics Grade 8: A Report Card for Ontario* (Toronto: Queen's Printer, 1991).

Chapter 7: Sharing Responsibility

1. London Council of Home and School Associations, *Elementary School Parents' Attitude Survey: Final Report*, April 1992, p. 31.

2. Ontario Teachers' Federation, *Beyond the Glitterspeak*, 1992 Submission to the (Ontario) Cabinet (Toronto: Ontario Teachers' Federation, 1992), p. i.

3. Ontario Teachers' Federation, op. cit., p. 40.

4. Harold Stevenson and James Stigler, *The Learning Gap* (New York: Summit Books, 1992) and Merry White, *The Japanese Educational Challenge: A Commitment to Children* (New York: The Free Press, 1987).

5. James Downey and Aldea Landry, *Schools for a New Century*, Report of the Commission on Excellence in Education (Fredericton: Government of New Brunswick, 1992), p. 9.

6. Cited by Stevenson and Stigler (op.cit.) from B. Watson, *Basic Writings of Mo Tzu, Hsun Tzu, and Han Fei Tzu* (New York: Columbia University Press, 1967), p. 18.

7. Toronto Board of Education, *The Effects of Parental Involvement on Children's Achievement*, research report (Toronto: Toronto Board of Education, 1987).

8. Merry White, op. cit. See, especially, Chapter 6.

9. Stevenson and Stigler, op. cit., p. 54. No comparative Canadian data are available.

10. Corporate-Higher Education Forum, *Learning Goals for K-12 Education: To Be Our Best* (Montreal: Corporate-Higher Education Forum, 1992).

11. The Business Roundtable, *Business Means Business About Education*, a synopsis of The Business Roundtable companies' education partnerships, New York, 1989, p.3.

12. Michael Bloom, *Profiles of Partnerships: Business-Education Partnerships that Enhance Student Retention* (Ottawa: Conference Board of Canada, 1991).

13. J. Myron Atkin and Ann Atkin, *Improving Science Education Through Local Alliances* (Santa Cruz, CA: ETR Associates, 1989).

14. Cooperative, Career and Work Education Association of Canada, private communication.

15. Marsha Levine, "Introduction" in Marsha Levine and Roberta Trachtman (eds.), *American Business and the Public School: Case Studies of Corporate Involvement in Public Education* (New York: Teachers College Press, 1988), p. xxii.

16. Statistics Canada, *Trends in the Family* (Ottawa: Statistics Canada, 1991), p. 39.

17. Robert Sexton, "School Reform Is Not a Spectator Sport," *Education Week*, October 28, 1992, p. 32.

18. Cindy Heine, *The School Answer Book: Citizens' Guide to Kentucky School Law* (Lexington, KY: Prichard Committee for Academic Excellence, 1992), p. 55.

19. Larry Martz, *Making Schools Better: How Parents and Teachers Across the Country Are Taking Action — And How You Can, Too* (New York: Times Books, 1992) p. xv.

Chapter 8: Learning from Experience

1. Peter Senge, *The Fifth Discipline: The Art and Practice of the Learning Organization* (New York: Doubleday, 1990), p. 18.

2. Ontario Teachers' Federation, *Teachers in Charge Newsletter*, Vol. 1, No. 1 (September 1992), p. 2.

3. For example, *Schools for a New Century*, Report of the Commission of Excellence in Education (Fredericton: Government of New Brunswick, 1992) and *Our Children, Our Future*, Report of the Royal Commission of Inquiry Into the Delivery of Programs and Services in Primary, Elementary, Secondary Education (St. John's: Government of Newfoundland and Labrador, 1992).

4. As documented, for example by Kathy O'Reilly Scanlon in *Tales Out of School* (Carp, Ontario: Creative Bound, 1992).

5. A.J.C. King and M.J. Peart, *Teachers in Canada: Their Work and Quality of Life* (Ottawa: Canadian Teachers' Federation, 1992), p. 120.

6. Similar ambivalence exists elsewhere. In the United States, for example, a growing literature on how to reform teacher education is, as yet, inconclusive. See, for example, Geraldine Clifford and James Guthrie, *Ed School* (Chicago: University of Chicago Press, 1988) and John Goodlad, *Teachers for Our Nation's Schools* (San Francisco: Jossey Bass, 1990). In Canada, the most significant study of teacher education has been by Michael Fullan and Michael Connelly, *Teacher Education in Ontario* (Toronto: Ontario Ministries of Education and Colleges and Universities, 1987).

7. B.B. Kymlicka et al., "Proposal for a New Direction: The Professional Education of Teachers as Graduate Studies," Unpublished report, University of Western Ontario Faculty of Education, February, 1993, p. 11.

8. Charles Ungerleider, "Power, Politics and Professionalism: The Impact of Change in British Columbia on the Status of Teachers and Their Professional Conduct," Unpublished paper, University of British Columbia, Department of Social and Educational Studies, 1991.

9. New Brunswick Commission on Excellence in Education, op. cit., p. 30.

10. Mary M. Schoeneberger, "Teaching Science at Seaward Elementary School," in John Olson and Thomas Russell, *Science Education in Canadian Schools: Case Studies of Science Teaching*, Science Council of Canada background Study 52 (Ottawa: Supply and Services Canada, 1984), p. 42.

11. Op. cit., p. 31.

12. Lewis Perelman, *School's Out: Hyperlearning, the New Technology and the End of Education* (New York: Morrow, 1992), pp. 215-22.

13. Stuart Smith, *Report of the Commission of Inquiry on Canadian University Education* (Ottawa: Association of Universities and Colleges of Canada, 1991), p. 90.

Chapter 9: A Call to Arms

1. Robert Sexton, "School Reform Is Not a Spectator Sport," *Education Week* (October 28, 1992), p. 32.

2. Edward B. Fiske, *Smart Schools, Smart Kids: Why Do Some Schools Work?* (New York: Touchstone, 1992), p. 235.

3. New York State Board of Regents, *A New Compact for Learning: Improving Public Elementary, Middle, and Secondary Education Results in the 1990s* (Albany: New York State Education Department, 1991).

4. California State Board of Education, *Summary of the Charter Schools Act* (Sacramento: California State Board of Education, 1993).

5. Department for Education, *Choice and Diversity: A New Framework for Schools* (London: Her Majesty's Stationery Office, 1992). An American account of the British reforms is provided by John E. Chubb and Terry M. Moe, *A Lesson in School Reform from Great Britain* (Washington: Brookings Institution, 1992).

6. Science Council of Canada, *Science for Every Student: Educating Canadians for Tomorrow's World* (Ottawa: Supply and Services Canada, 1984).

7. The Science Council's model, called "deliberative inquiry," is described in Graham Orpwood, "Toward the Renewal of Canadian Science Education: I. Deliberative Inquiry Model," *Science Education*, Vol. 69, No. 4 (July 1985), pp. 477-89.

Additional Reading

The following books released in Canada and the United States over the past few years reflect a variety of viewpoints on education reform. They do not represent a full bibliography, but are intended as a starting point for Canadians interested in exploring ideas about school reform.

Canada

Alberta Education. *Achieving Vision.* (Edmonton: Government of Alberta, 1991).

David Bender and Marc Forrest. *How to Help Your Child Achieve Success in School: A Parental Resource Book.* (Toronto: Ontario Public School Teacher's Federation, 1990).

Canadian School Boards Association. *Toward a Level Playing Field.* (Ottawa, 1992).

Canadian Teacher's Federation. *A Cappella: A Report on the Realities, Concerns, Expectations and Barriers Experienced by Adolescent Women in Canada.* (Ottawa, 1990).

Government of Canada Prosperity Initiative. *Canada's Prosperity: Challenges and Prospects.* (Ottawa, 1992).

Government of Canada Prosperity Initiative. *Inventing Our Future: An Action Plan for Canada's Prosperity.* (Ottawa, 1992).

Government of New Brunswick. *Schools for a New Century: Report of the Commission on Educational Excellence.* 1992.

Government of Newfoundland and Labrador. *Our Children, Our Future: Royal Commission of Inquiry into the Delivery of Programs and Services in Primary, Elementary, Secondary Education.* 1992.

Government of Quebec. *Joining Forces: Plan of Action on Educational Success.* 1992.

A.J.C. King and M.J. Peart. *Teachers in Canada: Their Work and Quality of Life.* (Ottawa: Canadian Teacher's Federation, 1992).

A.J.C. King and M.J. Peart. *The Good School.* (Toronto: The Ontario Secondary School Teacher's Federation, 1990).

Maryann McLaughlin. *Employability Skills Profile: What are Employers Looking for?* (Ottawa: Conference Board of Canada, 1992).

Nova Scotia Legislature. *Report of the Select Committee on Education.* (Halifax, March, 1992).

Ontario Premier's Council. *People and Skills in the New Global Economy.* (Toronto, 1990).

Jill Solnicki. *The Real Me is Gonna Be A Shock.* (Toronto: Lester Publishing Ltd., 1992).

Barry M. Sullivan. *A Legacy for Learners: The Report of the Royal Commission on Education.* (Province of British Columbia, 1988).

Toronto Board of Education. *The Young Adolescent Learner: Task Force V.* (Toronto, 1991).

United States

Mortimer J. Adler. *The Paideia Proposal: An Educational Manifesto.* (New York: Macmillan Publishing Co., 1982).

Mortimer J. Adler. *Paideia Problems and Possibilities.* (New York: Macmillan Publishing Co., 1983).

Samuel B. Bacharch (ed.). *Educational Reform: Making Sense of it All.* (Boston: Allyn and Bacon, 1990.)

Jack E. Bowsher. *Educating America: Lessons Learned in the Nation's Corporations.* (New York: John Wiley & Sons, 1989).

William Lowe Boyd and Herbert Walberg (eds.). *Choice in Education: Potential and Problems.* (Berkeley, CA: McCutcheon, 1990).

John E. Chubb and Terry M. Moe. *Politics, Markets & America's Schools.* (Washington: The Brookings Institution, 1990).

John E. Chubb and Terry M. Moe. *A Lesson in School Reform from Great Britain.* (Washington: The Brookings Institution, 1990).

Thomas W. Evans. *Mentors: Making a Difference in Our Public Schools.* (Princeton, N.J.: Peterson's Guides, 1992).

Edward B. Fiske. *Smart Schools, Smart Kids: Why Do Some Schools Work?* (New York: Touchstone Books, 1992).

Patricia Albjerg Graham. *SOS: Sustain Our Schools.* (New York: Hill and Wang, 1992).

G. Alfred Hess. *School Restructuring, Chicago Style.* (Newbury Park, CA: Corwin Press, 1991).

David T. Kearns and Denis P. Doyle. *Winning the Brain Race: A Bold Plan to Make Our Schools Competitive,* revised edition. (San Francisco: ICS Press, 1991).

Johnathan Kozol. *Savage Inequalities: Children in America's Schools.* (New York: Crown Publishers, 1991).

Marsha Levine and Roberta Trachtman (eds.) *American Business and the Public School: Case Studies of Corporate Involvement in Public Education.* (New York: Teachers College Press, 1989).

Lawrence W. Lezotte. *Creating the Total Quality Effective School.* (Okemos, Michigan: Effective School Products, 1992).

Ray Marshall and Marc Tucker. *Thinking for a Living: Education and the Wealth of Nations.* New York: Basic Books, 1992).

Larry Martz. *Making Schools Better: How Parents and Teachers Across the Country Are Taking Action — and How You Can, Too.* (New York: Times Books, 1992).

William E. Nothdurft. *SchoolWorks: Reinventing Public Schools to Create the Workforce of the Future, Innovations in Education and Job Training from Sweden, West Germany, Great Britain, France . . . and Philadelphia.* (Washington: The Brookings Institution, 1980).

David Osborne and Ted Gaebler. *Reinventing Government: How the Entrepreneurial Spirit is Transforming the Public Sector from Schoolhouse to Statehouse, City Hall to the Pentagon.* (New York: Addison-Wesley, 1992.)

Lewis J. Perelman. *School's Out: Hyperlearning, the New Technology, and the End of Education.* (New York: William Morrow, 1992).

Philip C. Schlechty. *Schools for the 21st Century: Leadership Imperatives for Educational Reform.* (San Francisco: Jossey-Bass, 1991).

Theodore R. Sizer. *Horace's School: Redesigning the American High School.* (Boston: Houghton Mifflin, 1984).

Theodore R. Sizer. *Horace's Compromise: The Dilemma of the American High School.* (Boston: Houghton Mifflin, 1984).

Harold Stevenson and James Stigler. *The Learning Gap: Why Our Schools Are Failing and What We Can Learn from the Japanese and Chinese Education.* (New York: Summit Books, 1992).

Thomas Toch. *In the Name of Excellence: The Struggle to Reform the Nation's Schools, Why It's Failing and What Should be Done.* (New York: Oxford University Press, 1991).

Merry White. *The Japanese Educational Challenge: A Commitment to Children.* (New York: The Free Press, 1987).

Additional Contacts

The governments and organizations listed below are useful starting points for additional information on policies and programs in education across Canada.

Governments

British Columbia
Ministry of Education
Parliament Buildings
Victoria, British Columbia
V8V 2M4
Minister: Anita Hagen
(604) 387-4611

Alberta
Ministry of Education
West Tower, Devonian Building
11160 Jasper Ave.
Edmonton, Alberta
T5K 0L2
Minister: Halver Jonson
(403) 427-2025

Saskatchewan
Ministry of Education
2220 College Avenue
Regina, Saskatchewan
S4P 2V7
Minister: Carol Teichrob
(306) 787-7360

Ontario
Ministry of Education and
   Training
Mowat Block, 900 Bay St.
Toronto, Ontario
M7A 1L2
Minister: Dave Cooke
(416) 325-2600

New Brunswick
Department of Education
P.O. Box 6000
Fredericton, New Brunswick
E3B 5H1
Minister: Paul Duffie
(506) 453-3678

Prince Edward Island
Department of Education
Box 2000
Shaw Building, 4th Floor
95 Rochford St.
Charlottetown, Prince Edward
   Island
C1A 7N8
Minister: Paul Connolly
(902) 368-4600

Manitoba
Department of Education and
   Training
Legislative Bldg.
Winnipeg, Manitoba
R3C 0V9
Minister: Rosemary Vodrey
(204) 945-2211

Québec
Ministère de l'Education
Edifice Marie-Guyart
1035, rue de la Chevrotière
Québec, Québec
G1R 5A5
Ministère: Lucienne Robillard
(418) 643-7095

Nova Scotia
Department of Education
Box 578
Halifax, Nova Scotia
B3J 2S9
Minister: Guy Le Blanc
(902) 424-5605

Newfoundland
Department of Education
Box 8700
St. John's, Newfoundland
A1B 4J6
Minister: Chris Decker
(709) 729-2466

Northwest Territories
Department of Education, Culture
   and Employment Programs
P.O. Box 1320
Yellowknife, Northwest Territories
X1A 2L9
Minister: James Arvauluk
(403) 873-7529

Yukon
Department of Education
P.O. Box 2703
Whitehorse, Yukon Territory
Y1A 2C6
Minister: Douglas Phillips
(403) 667-5141

**Council of Ministers of Education
  of Canada**
252 Bloor St. W.
Suite 5-200
Toronto, Ontario
M5S 1V5
(416) 964-2551

Federal Government
Stay in School Initiative
Department of Employment
   and Immigration
Phase IV
Place du Portage
Hull, Québec
K1A 0J9

Steering Group on Prosperity
Ottawa, Ontario
K1A 0H5
(613) 941-2451

National Organizations

Canada Education Association
252 Bloor St. W.
Toronto, Ontario
M5S 1V5
(416) 924-7721

**Canadian Home and School and
  Parent-Teacher Federation**
331 Somerset St. W.
Ottawa, Ontario
K2P 0J8
(613) 232-7292

**Organization for Quality
  Education**
P.O. Box 472
Station U
Etobicoke, Ontario
M8Z 5Y8
(416) 252-6009

**Canadian Catholic School
  Trustees' Association**
80 Sheppard Ave. E.
Toronto, Ontario
M2N 6E8

Skills Canada
80 Bradford St., Unit 23G
Barrie, Ontario
L4N 6S7
(705) 734-9170

**Canadian School Boards'
  Association**
Suite 600
130 Slater St.
Ottawa, Ontario
K1P 6E2

Canadian Teachers' Federation
110 Argyle Ave.
Ottawa, Ontario
K2P 1B4
(613) 232-1886

Business Groups with Education Programs

Conference Board of Canada
National Business and Education
  Centre
255 Smyth Road
Ottawa, Ontario
K1H 8M7

**Corporate-Higher Education
  Forum**
1155 Rene-Levesque Blvd. W.
Suite 2501
Montréal, Québec
H3B 2K4
(514) 876-1356

**Canadian Federation of
  Independent Business**
4141 Yonge St.
Toronto, Ontario
M2P 2A8
(416) 222-8022

Faculties of Education at:

University of Alberta
Edmonton, Alberta
T6G 2E1
(403) 492-3751

University of British Columbia
2075 Wesbrook Mall
Vancouver, B.C.
(604) 822-5211

Brock University
Merrittville Highway
St. Catharines, Ontario
(416) 688-5550 ext. 3710

University of Calgary
2500 University Dr. N.
Calgary, Alberta
(403) 220-5627

Dalhousie University
Halifax, N.S.
(902) 494-2319

Ecole des Hautes Etudes
5255, avenue Decelles
Montréal, Québec
H3T 1V6
(514) 340-6333

Lakehead University
Oliver Road
Thunder Bay, Ontario
P7B 5E1
(807) 343-8023 ext. 8199

University of Manitoba
Winnipeg, Manitoba
R3T 2N2
(204) 474-9001

McGill University
845 Sherbrooke St. W.
Montréal, Québec
H3A 2T5
(514) 398-7038

Memorial University
Elizabeth Avenue
St. John's, Newfoundland
A1C 5S7
(709) 737-8588

Université de Montréal
C.P. 6128
Succursale A
Montréal, Québec
H3C 3J7
(514) 343-6761

Mount Allison University
Sackville, New Brunswick
E0A 3C0
(506) 364-2520

Mount Saint Vincent
Halifax, Nova Scotia
B3M 2J6
(902) 443-4450 ext. 341

**Ontario Institute for Studies
  in Education**
252 Bloor St. W.
Toronto, Ontario
M5V 1V5
(416) 923-6641

University of Prince Edward Island
550 University Ave.
Charlottetown, P.E.I.
C1A 4P3
(902) 566-0349

University of Regina
Regina, Saskatchewan
S4S 0A2
(306) 585-4500

Simon Fraser University
Burnaby, B.C.
V5A 1S6
(604) 291-3148

University of Victoria
P.O. Box 1700
Victoria, B.C.
V8W 2Y2
(604) 721-8611

University of Windsor
401 Sunset Ave.
Windsor, Ontario
N9B 3P4
(519) 253-3913

University of New Brunswick
P.O. Box 4400
Fredericton, N.B.
E3B 5A3
(506) 453-4862

University of Ottawa
1 Nicholas St.
Ottawa, Ontario
K1N 6N5
(613) 564-5444

Queen's University
Kingston, Ontario
K7L 3N6
(613) 545-6210

University of Saskatchewan
Saskatoon, Saskatchewan
S7N 0W0
(306) 966-7647

University of Toronto
Toronto, Ontario
M5S 1A1
(416) 978-3223

University of Western Ontario
London, Ontario
N6A 3K7
(519) 661-2080

York University
4700 Keele St.
North York, Ontario
M3J 1P3
(416) 736-5002

Index